New Directions in Book History

Series Editors
Shafquat Towheed
Faculty of Arts
Open University
Milton Keynes, UK

Jonathan Rose
Department of History
Drew University
Madison, NJ, USA

As a vital field of scholarship, book history has now reached a stage of maturity where its early work can be reassessed and built upon. That is the goal of New Directions in Book History. This series will publish monographs in English that employ advanced methods and open up new frontiers in research, written by younger, mid-career, and senior scholars. Its scope is global, extending to the Western and non-Western worlds and to all historical periods from antiquity to the 21st century, including studies of script, print, and post-print cultures. New Directions in Book History, then, will be broadly inclusive but always in the vanguard. It will experiment with inventive methodologies, explore unexplored archives, debate overlooked issues, challenge prevailing theories, study neglected subjects, and demonstrate the relevance of book history to other academic fields. Every title in this series will address the evolution of the historiography of the book, and every one will point to new directions in book scholarship. New Directions in Book History will be published in three formats: single-author monographs; edited collections of essays in single or multiple volumes; and shorter works produced through Palgrave's e-book (EPUB2) 'Pivot' stream. Book proposals should emphasize the innovative aspects of the work, and should be sent to either of the two series editors.

Editorial Board
Marcia Abreu, University of Campinas, Brazil
Cynthia Brokaw, Brown University, USA
Matt Cohen, University of Texas at Austin, USA
Archie Dick, University of Pretoria, South Africa
Martyn Lyons, University of New South Wales, Australia

More information about this series at
http://www.palgrave.com/gp/series/14749

Lara Atkin • Sarah Comyn
Porscha Fermanis • Nathan Garvey

Early Public Libraries and Colonial Citizenship in the British Southern Hemisphere

palgrave
macmillan

Lara Atkin
University College Dublin
Dublin, Ireland

Sarah Comyn
University College Dublin
Dublin, Ireland

Porscha Fermanis
University College Dublin
Dublin, Ireland

Nathan Garvey
University College Dublin
Dublin, Ireland

New Directions in Book History
ISBN 978-3-030-20425-9   ISBN 978-3-030-20426-6   (eBook)
https://doi.org/10.1007/978-3-030-20426-6

© The Editor(s) (if applicable) and The Author(s) 2019. This book is an open access publication.

Open Access This book is licensed under the terms of the Creative Commons Attribution 4.0 International License (http://creativecommons.org/licenses/by/4.0/), which permits use, sharing, adaptation, distribution and reproduction in any medium or format, as long as you give appropriate credit to the original author(s) and the source, provide a link to the Creative Commons licence and indicate if changes were made.

The images or other third party material in this book are included in the book's Creative Commons licence, unless indicated otherwise in a credit line to the material. If material is not included in the book's Creative Commons licence and your intended use is not permitted by statutory regulation or exceeds the permitted use, you will need to obtain permission directly from the copyright holder.

The use of general descriptive names, registered names, trademarks, service marks, etc. in this publication does not imply, even in the absence of a specific statement, that such names are exempt from the relevant protective laws and regulations and therefore free for general use.

The publisher, the authors and the editors are safe to assume that the advice and information in this book are believed to be true and accurate at the date of publication. Neither the publisher nor the authors or the editors give a warranty, express or implied, with respect to the material contained herein or for any errors or omissions that may have been made. The publisher remains neutral with regard to jurisdictional claims in published maps and institutional affiliations.

Cover illustration: History and Art Collection / Alamy Stock Photo

This Palgrave Pivot imprint is published by the registered company Springer Nature Switzerland AG
The registered company address is: Gewerbestrasse 11, 6330 Cham, Switzerland

Acknowledgements

This research was funded by the European Research Council under the Horizon 2020 research and innovation programme (grant agreement no. 679436), and the authors would like to thank the Council for its generosity. We must also acknowledge our great debt to the following open access databases containing digital surrogates of important nineteenth-century sources: National Library of Australia's Trove database; National Library of Singapore's NewspaperSG database; National Library of New Zealand's Papers Past database; Internet Archive; and SouthHem's Book Catalogues of the Colonial Southern Hemisphere (BCCSH) digital archive.

Detailed acknowledgements of the various individuals and institutions who provided valuable assistance during the preparation of the BCCSH digital archive are available on the SouthHem website: http://www.ucd.ie/southhem/acknowledgments.html. At Palgrave Macmillan, we would like to thank Allie Troyanos, Rachel Jacobe, and Ben Doyle. Our anonymous peer reviewers provided excellent suggestions and guidance, for which we are grateful. We would also like to thank colleagues at University College Dublin for their support, in particular, John Brannigan, Andrew Carpenter, Danielle Clarke, Lucy Cogan, Nick Daly, Sharae Deckard, Margaret Kelleher, Amanda Nettelbeck, Michelle O'Connell, Eoin O'Mahoney, and Sarah Sharp. Special thanks must go to Kaitlin Picard, our visiting research assistant from the University of Rhode Island, for her assistance with statistics relating to catalogue holdings. Finally, we would like to thank James Raven for his encouragement and inspiration.

Attributions

This book is the result of a collaborative research project, and its ideas and arguments have been jointly conceived. Each chapter was nonetheless written by a lead author or authors and, for the purposes of research assessment, the following attribution of authorship is acknowledged: Chap. 1 (Fermanis); Chap. 2 (Fermanis and Garvey); Chap. 3 (Comyn and Fermanis); Chap. 4 (Comyn); Chap. 5 (Atkin); and Chap. 6 (Atkin and Fermanis). Primary and archival research is attributed in the following manner: ASL and TPL (Garvey); MPL (Comyn); SAI (Fermanis); SAPL (Atkin); and SL and RLM (Fermanis).

Referencing

Citations from the Book Catalogues of the Colonial Southern Hemisphere (BCCSH) digital archive give both the short title of the catalogue and a URL linking directly to the digital surrogate of the catalogue. Each catalogue entered into the archive has its own unique record. All records are correct as of 11 March 2019.

European Research Council
Established by the European Commission

Praise for *Early Public Libraries and Colonial Citizenship in the British Southern Hemisphere*

"*Early Public Libraries and Colonial Citizenship in the British Southern Hemisphere* is an important contribution to the study of library history, an often over looked aspect of the history of the book [or *histoire de livre*]. The four co-authors provide a scholarly and readable comparative study of the role major public libraries played in the nineteenth century in community building and the public sphere in British colonies south of the equator."

—John Arnold, *Affiliate, Faculty of Arts, Monash University, Australia, and co-editor of* A History of the Book in Australia 1891–1945, A National Culture in a Colonised Market *(2001)*

Contents

1 Introduction — 1

2 From Community to Public Libraries: Liberalism, Education, and Self-Government — 17

3 Cultivating Public Readers: Citizens, Classes, and Types — 45

4 'A mob of light readers': Holdings, Genre Proportions, and Modes of Reading — 77

5 Knowing the 'Native Mind': Ethnological and Philological Collections — 103

6 Conclusion — 127

Appendix A: Explanatory Note on Catalogue Sources — 139

Appendix B: Volume Numbers of Colonial Public Libraries — 143

Appendix C: Genre Proportions of Colonial Public Libraries by Title	145

Select Bibliography	149

Index	153

Abbreviations

ALSMI	Adelaide Literary Society and Mechanics' Institute
ASL	Australian Subscription Library
BML	British Museum Library
FPL	Free Public Library
JIA	*Journal of the Indian Archipelago and Eastern Asia*
JSBRAS	*Journal of the Straits Branch of the Royal Asiatic Society*
MPL	Melbourne Public Library
RLM	Raffles Library and Museum
SAI	South Australian Institute
SALMI	South Australian Library and Mechanics' Institute
SAM	South African Museum
SAPL	South African Public Library
SAQJ	*South African Quarterly Journal*
SI	South African Institute
SL	Singapore Library
TPL	Tasmanian Public Library

List of Figures

Fig. 2.1 'Uses of a Public Library', *Melbourne Punch*, August 2, 1855, 153. Courtesy of Trove: https://trove.nla.gov.au/newspaper/article/171430414 — 18

Fig. 2.2 Samuel Calvert, 'The Reading Room of the Melbourne Public Library', wood engraving, *Illustrated Melbourne Post*, June 27, 1866. Courtesy of the State Library of Victoria: http://handle.slv.vic.gov.au/10381/295506 — 32

Fig. 3.1 'While There's Life There's Soap', wood engraving, *Melbourne Punch*, January 13, 1887, 15. Courtesy of Trove: https://trove.nla.gov.au/newspaper/page/20442557 — 57

Fig. 3.2 'At the Public Library', wood engraving, *Australasian Sketcher*, February 23, 1888, Courtesy of the State Library of Victoria: http://handle.slv.vic.gov.au/10381/258786 — 60

Fig. 3.3 'Synopsis of the Public Library', *Catalogue*, MPL, 1861, xvi. Courtesy of BCCSH and the State Library of Victoria: http://www.ucd.ie/southhem/record.html#112 — 64

LIST OF TABLES

Table C.1	SL and RLM	145
Table C.2	SAI	145
Table C.3	SAPL	146
Table C.4	ASL	146
Table C.5	TPL	146
Table C.6	MPL	147

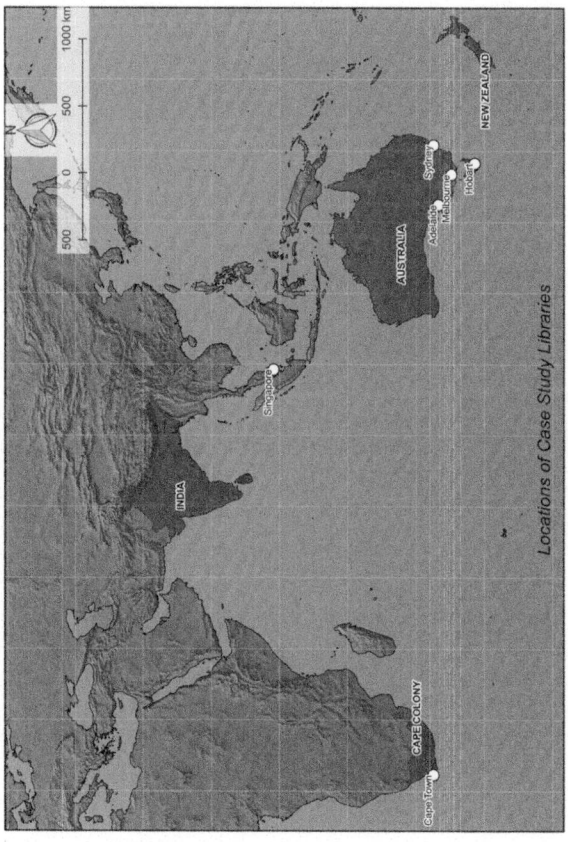

Fig. 1 Map 'Location of Case Study Libraries', based on Walter Crane, 'Imperial Federation: Map Showing the Extent of the British Empire in 1886', colour lithograph, *The Graphic*, July 24, 1886. Courtesy of the Norman B. Leventhal Map Centre Collection via Wikimedia Commons: https://commons.wikimedia.org/wiki/File:Imperial_Federation,_map_of_the_world_showing_the_extent_of_the_British_Empire_in_1886.jpg

CHAPTER 1

Introduction

Abstract This introduction outlines the primary arguments and methodologies of the book, including new imperial history models, networked conceptualisations of empire, and comparative and transnational history. It argues both for the existence of transnational institutional connections and reading audiences across the colonial southern hemisphere, and for the importance of local and regional variations in the reproduction of the British public library model. It concludes by outlining the book's primary sources, as well as introducing its six case study libraries from colonial Australia, South Africa, and Southeast Asia.

Keywords Library studies • Book history • Public libraries • Catalogues • Southern hemisphere

This book traces the emergence of public libraries from within a flourishing, but uncoordinated and often precarious, culture of community and commercial libraries in the British colonial southern hemisphere and Straits Settlements in the nineteenth century. Once dismissed as an aspect of provincial attempts to create 'Little Britains' in the colonies by replicating metropolitan institutions and standards of taste, the colonial public library is now understood as a major nineteenth-century cultural phenomenon that did much more than simply supply books to readers.[1] For the 'southern colonies',[2] the public library became richly symbolic of various

© The Author(s) 2019
L. Atkin et al., *Early Public Libraries and Colonial Citizenship in the British Southern Hemisphere*, New Directions in Book History,
https://doi.org/10.1007/978-3-030-20426-6_1

types of proto-national cultural self-assertion, as well as providing an institutional framework for a range of intersecting ideological disputes, from debates about self-governance and citizenship, to racial hierarchies and the acculturation of Indigenous peoples, to questions of taste and cultural capital. Colonial readers, too, were much more than just passive recipients of books imported from Britain and other metropolitan centres, instead selecting, consuming, and interpreting texts in diverse and often locally specific ways.

Moving away from institutional library history towards a cultural and social history of the library,[3] this book asks a series of critical questions. What roles did early public libraries play in colonial societies? How did these roles vary or converge across different colonial spaces? Who were the reading publics addressed and enabled by public libraries? And how did the public library provide a forum or opportunity for various forms of identity formation, and knowledge production and dissemination? By looking at these questions within a particular historical and geographical context—from Singapore to Cape Town to Melbourne—one of the book's primary aims is to assess the degree of cross-fertilisation between early colonial public libraries and their users. A second aim is to think about these libraries at various levels of scale from the discrete local conditions that shaped their establishment to wider global developments in library provision. A third aim is to consider the ways in which early public libraries contributed to the self-fashioning of colonial identities and polities in the nineteenth-century Anglophone world.

Drawing on James Belich's influential 'Anglo-divergence' model of the nineteenth-century settler explosion,[4] we argue that the colonial public library helped to create reading publics that reflected the shared, but also locally distinct, civic identities of multiple emerging colonial states in Australia, the Cape Colony, and the Straits Settlements. In the case of the Cape Colony and Singapore, public libraries also played an important role in establishing the cultural hegemony of an Anglophone literary culture that worked in tandem with efforts to anglicise administrative and legal systems in previously Dutch spheres of influence, as well as helping to institutionalise the ethnographic and philological knowledge that underwrote increasingly racialised colonial social orders. At the same time, such libraries addressed and engaged with public spheres that transcended their colony's 'national' boundaries and Anglophone linguistic cultures, from regional networks of readers, collectors, and associational groups, to longer-range interactions with metropolitan institutions, continental European collecting cultures, and global émigré and diaspora communities. If these connections did not necessarily result in a fully articulated transcolonial or transnational reading public,[5] they nonetheless point to the existence of shared practices and experiences of reading, collecting, and archiving across and beyond the Anglosphere world. Examining these kinds of cosmopolitan mind-sets and transnational connections, as well as the international flows of knowledge they enabled, allows us to 'recast national histories' and their 'long traditions of exceptionalism', while simultaneously throwing into relief the central role that public libraries played in shaping questions of colonial nationhood in the nineteenth century.[6]

BEYOND A NATIONAL HISTORY OF THE LIBRARY

With the notable exception of transatlantic studies, there has been little sustained attempt to consider the formation of colonial libraries comparatively across different national, geographic, and linguistic borders. The reasons for this range from the field's methodological 'predilection for the micro-historical case study' to the prevalence of nation-centred library histories.[7] As Robb Haberman and Lynda Yankaskas's work on provincial nationalism has shown us, the 'library project … was explicitly part of nation-building, a tool to create a new citizenry for a new country', but studies of the nature of nation-building have increasingly rejected any easy separation between nationalism and globalism.[8] At the same time, comparative approaches tend to shore up national boundaries. Marilyn Lake has rightly noted that while comparative history has 'opened up questions about national distinctiveness', the effect of comparativism is often to 'present parallel histories that reinforce the dominance of national paradigms'.[9] An openness to transnational frameworks, and the ways in which ideas, peoples, and practices cross national borders, is especially important in a period in which various incipient forms of nationhood, from responsible government to federation, were not yet solidified.

By considering several colonial public libraries in both a comparative and a transnational context, this book seeks to uncover their communalities and connections, looking for patterns across acquisition policies, library holdings, and readerships, while also acknowledging the local variations that enable fruitful intercolonial and transcolonial comparison. In so doing, the book forms part of a wider theoretical imperative in imperial studies that seeks to question received understandings of the relationship between metropole and colony. Shifting attention away from both metropolitan and national histories of empire in favour of 'new imperial history' paradigms that privilege imbricated national and imperial 'intercultures', circuits and networks, and regional hubs or nodal points,[10] this study claims for the public libraries of the southern colonies a historical and spatial specificity made up of particularly dense south–south networks of readers, and exchanges of books, information, and ideas.[11]

Most obviously, British settlements in the southern hemisphere were linked by relative proximity, geo-political interests, imperial shipping and trade routes, global mass media networks, and communication technologies.[12] Another point of connection was provided by overlapping and intra-generational networks of settlers, administrators, missionaries, ethnographers, collectors, and bibliophiles, such as George Grey, James Richardson Logan, and Redmond Barry, whose colonial careers and socio-material networks traversed colonial Australia, New Zealand, British India, the Cape Colony, and the Straits Settlements, and whose bibliophiliac zeal linked libraries in Melbourne, Auckland, Singapore, the Cape, and Britain. But while the idea of empire as a networked space of circuits and flows is critical for understanding how information circulated within imperial spaces, it is also possible to write a history of colonial intellectual life that focuses less on well-known intellectuals and administrators, and more on the institutional 'processes through which knowledge was produced and consumed'.[13] The public library, we argue, is an important example of this kind of 'intellectual infrastructure', providing not only a nodal point for intersecting groups of people, but also a way of understanding how colonial communities created, accessed, categorised, and disseminated different forms of knowledge.[14]

We are interested both in the 'stratigraphic' approach to collections—that is, how they are built up over time via various social agents and mediators—and in the ways in which book holdings overlap and diverge across the region. If there is some uniformity among the holdings of colonial public libraries in terms of genre proportions and titles stocked (particularly in relation to fiction holdings), there is also great variety in the ways in which such libraries approached local material, reference collections, and the archiving process. Public-sphere debates about the collections formed by early colonial public libraries suggest shared tensions across the southern colonies between the demands of competing colonial reading publics and social classes (Chap. 3), the need to provide both 'light' recreational reading and 'serious' reference collections (Chap. 4), and the enlightenment universalist aspirations of the 'national' collection and the desire to promote local archival collection and ethnographic field work (Chap. 5).

This book focuses on these three transcolonial public-sphere debates. While class tensions and the so-called 'fiction problem' were a concern for all the libraries under consideration, the extensive ethnological and philological collections of the South African Public Library (SAPL) and the Raffles Library and Museum (RLM) were not replicated in Australian and New Zealand public libraries until large bequests to the State Library of New South Wales and the Auckland Public Library in 1907 and 1886, respectively. Demographic factors provide one explanation for this divergence. In contrast to colonial Australia and New Zealand, where by 1860 the booming European settler populations far outnumbered Indigenous populations, European settlers were always a minority in Singapore and the Cape Colony.[15] By the mid-nineteenth century, Europeans made up less than 3% of the general population in Singapore and around 37% in the Cape.[16] In these white minority settlements, local knowledge collection was particularly critical to the broader project of regulating Indigenous and colonial conduct that David Scott has termed 'colonial governmentality'.[17] The Logan and Grey bequests, considered in detail in Chap. 5, were therefore manifestations of a wider scientific interest in ethnological and philological knowledge collection that developed in the Cape Colony and Singapore from the 1820s and 1840s, respectively. As well as classifying, categorising, and providing an institutional home for these large bequests, we argue that the SAPL and the RLM played a crucial role in fostering those learned societies and journals that concentrated on ethnographic and philological collection, thereby establishing themselves as regional centres of local knowledge creation and dissemination, and helping to institutionalise ethnology as a scientific discipline outside of metropolitan Europe.

Another key focus of the book is on the types of readers enabled by colonial public libraries, and on the ways in which reading practices were shaped by social patterns, literacy rates, and demographics (see Chaps. 3 and 4). As Julieanne Lamond has argued, library data is invaluable for studying communities of readers, first because libraries 'are social institutions whose primary rationale is reading' but also because the library is a 'physical space' representing reading communities 'defined by physical proximity and social relationships'. Libraries therefore create communities of readers, both in the sense of 'imagined communities' and 'real' or actual communities.[18] Real readers do not, of course, always 'play along with the founding principles of an institution' or 'follow the design outlined in catalogues'.[19] But imagined communities of readers are not so much 'fictitious consumers' or even 'ideal' readers, but rather 'ideational' readers, who correspond both to concrete forms of civic identity formation and to the performative world-making discourses that accompany the creation of reading publics.[20] Although we must be wary of 'crude and instrumentalist' mappings of book collections onto perceived reading communities,[21] this book argues that the readers imagined, created, and addressed by those responsible for assembling the collections of colonial public libraries are critical for understanding how colonial societies positioned themselves in relation to wider communities of knowledge.

Catalogues and Other Sources

While drawing on a variety of archival records and sources, the primary sources of evidence for this book are the printed catalogues of those colonial institutions that would later become major public libraries in the British southern hemisphere. Faced with an absence of consistent or ongoing records relating to borrowing and circulation, our focus on the catalogue in part reflects the fact that only lists of book holdings provide the required levels of statistical comparability across various colonial libraries in the nineteenth century. However, we also argue for the importance of the catalogue in thinking about books and readers at a structural or systemic level, that is, in thinking about patterns of holdings and acquisitions. Wallace Kirsop has rightly warned of the dangers of theorising about readers and public taste based on 'the bare facts of availability', but the surviving printed catalogues of colonial public libraries constitute a relatively fulsome source material in comparison to other types of catalogues, providing us with a snapshot of the nature of public library collections, and the books that were considered 'acquisition worthy', at various points in time (see Appendix A).[22]

Leah Price has noted that much recent work on the history of reading has focused on textual consumption, arguing that this neglects the ways in which texts can act as markers of prestige and ritual, and even as 'carriers of relationships'.[23] Of interest to this study are the various social and civic functions of public library catalogues, as well as the ways in which these functions are displayed in the catalogues themselves as material objects. Quite apart from being invaluable guides to library holdings, the design of catalogues, whether classical or divided by subject or format, allows us insights into a library's objectives, intentions, and usage, including the relative importance of different genres or categories of literature. Similarly, the uses and abuses of books—those that are uncut, dog-eared, thumbed over, annotated, or simply worn-out—may provide insights into readers' choices, tastes, and values.

Catalogues are, of course, also sites of disciplinary formation and transformation, enabling us to see the ways in which various types of knowledge—especially racialised forms of knowledge—were ordered, codified, and archived in the colonial world, as well as facilitating other sorts of intellectual endeavour such as society publishing and scholarly journals. As 'carefully curated' sites of colonial cultural capital,[24] prestige catalogues, such as the early catalogues of the Melbourne Public Library (MPL), served as a reminder of colonial progress via sophisticated illustrations, engravings, and plates of 'native' flora and fauna, which were intended to 'stamp' the library's character 'as a National Institution'.[25] These sorts of catalogues amounted to transportable emissaries of both the library and the colony itself, a function that was amplified through various forms of publication exchange and gifts of specially bound editions that were distributed to associations and government departments in Britain and elsewhere (see Chaps. 4 and 5). The role of the catalogue in reflecting colonial cultural aspirations and values, and in disseminating knowledge acquired in the colonies into the heart of transatlantic and continental European intellectual networks, makes it an important but undervalued means of understanding how information circulated globally in the nineteenth century.

Despite the richness of catalogues as source material, one of the challenging aspects of this study has been reconciling the different methods of classifying books between (and sometimes within) the institutions under consideration. While there is considerable variation in both the classificatory methods and the level of bibliographic detail provided by our library catalogues, all of them, with the exception of the early Australian Subscription Library (ASL) catalogues, offer analytical contents pages and/or indexes dividing their collections into distinct classes. These range in granularity from the MPL's 1860 catalogue, where 127 separate subject classes are listed in the classificatory index, to as few as eight classes in the SAPL's catalogues from 1829 onwards. Alexander Johnstone Jardine, then librarian at the SAPL and by far the most systematic of the colonial librarians in our case studies, adapted the subject classes recommended in the four-volume third edition of French bibliographer Jacques-Charles Brunet's influential *Manuel du Libraire* (1820), as well as being influenced by the classificatory system of the catalogues of the London Institution (est. 1805, later the Royal Institution),[26] namely, 'Theology and Divinity';

'Jurisprudence, Government and Politics'; 'Sciences and the Arts'; 'Surgery, Medicine and Chemistry'; 'Mathematics'; 'Belles Lettres'; 'History'; and 'Foreign Languages'.

In Chap. 4, our comparative analysis of book holdings is divided into seven broad categories: 'Science'; 'Political Economy, Politics and Jurisprudence'; 'Theology and Ethics'; 'Biography and History'; 'Geography, Voyages and Travels'; 'Imaginative Literature'; and 'Other' (see Appendix C).[27] In devising these categories, we have broadly followed Jardine's scheme as the one that best reflects shared classificatory categories across the case study libraries, but with three important qualifications. First, we have divided 'History' into 'Biography and History' and 'Geography, Voyages and Travels', both to reflect the modern disciplinary distinction between 'History' and 'Geography', and to better account for those libraries whose catalogues increasingly distinguish between the two disciplines. Second, our 'Science' category includes the natural sciences and mathematics, but excludes the mechanical arts and applied sciences on the basis that such categories were not generally classified as 'science' in the nineteenth century. Finally, we use 'Imaginative Literature' as a category that encompasses fiction, drama, and poetry but excludes *belles lettres* and critical works. This category enables us to consider the proportion of imaginative works (particularly fiction) in the holdings of our case study libraries. *Belles lettres* and modern languages have both been grouped with other smaller genres, such as fine arts and philology, into our 'Other' section, as the holdings of these categories across our case study libraries were small.

Case Studies, Models, and Precedents

The book's comparative case studies include the SAPL (est. 1818); the MPL (est. 1854); the South Australian Institute (SAI) (est. 1856); the Tasmanian Public Library (TPL) (est. 1849; 1869); the Free Public Library (FPL) (est. 1869); and the RLM (est. 1874). These at least partially publicly funded libraries have been selected on the basis that each of them established a relatively substantial reference collection in the nineteenth century and subsequently developed into a major 'national' library. By 1875, only three of the above libraries could be considered 'public' in the modern sense of being freely open to the general public and funded primarily by public money: the MPL, the TPL, and the FPL. Of these, only the FPL was a municipal library created through centralised legislation. While they had small lending branches for country readers, the MPL, the TPL, and the FPL were reference-only libraries. The remaining libraries had publicly accessible reference sections and reading rooms, but retained the user-pays subscription model for book borrowing.

The chronological focus of this study lies primarily between the 1810s and the 1870s, that is, the dates of establishment of the libraries under investigation. While in the Cape Colony public library provision began as early as 1818, the key decades for the emergence of public libraries in the Australian colonies are the 1850s and 1860s, and in the Straits Settlements the 1870s. Much of our comparative analysis therefore focuses on the period between 1850 and 1880, but we also consider important contextual material in the periods before and after those decades, for example, the development of the ethnographic collections of the RLM in the 1880s. New Zealand's first free public library, the Port Nicholson Exchange and Public Library, opened in Wellington in 1841 for only a year. Despite having three major libraries in the 1840s and Public Libraries Acts in 1869 and 1877, there was no enduring public library in colonial New Zealand until the Auckland Free Public Library (est. 1880), which was supported and sustained by a gift in 1887 of rare books, manuscripts, and ephemera from Sir George Grey, previously a Governor and Premier of New Zealand.[28] Grey's contribution to the development of the SAPL will be discussed in detail in Chap. 5, but the chronology for the emergence of major public libraries in the New Zealand colonies falls outside the timeframe of this study, which focuses on early public library provision.

In the southern colonies, public libraries drew on a variety of institutional, classificatory, and physical precedents—from the athenaeum to the mechanics' institute to the 'national' reference library—but for the most part they were based on British rather than North American or European institutions. Modelled on the London Institution, an athenaeum with a substantial reference library and laboratory, the SAPL was originally funded by a tax on the wine trade and was open free of charge to all inhabitants and visitors over the age of sixteen to Cape Town between 1822 and 1829.[29] After 1829, when government funding was withdrawn, the library was converted from a public library to a subscription library, radically altering the library's book-selection policies.[30] Prior to the completion of the Suez Canal in 1869, the Cape of Good Hope's position as a refresher station en route to India made the Cape Colony an important staging post for East India Company employees on leave from Company service. The patronage of these 'India visitors' was vital to the establishment and maintenance of the SAPL as one of the leading colonial libraries of the mid-nineteenth century.[31]

The SAPL remained committed to building up and maintaining a serious reference collection of scientific works from the 1820s onwards.[32] Between 1824 and 1848, the SAPL was supplied by the London bookseller James Malcott Richardson, and from 1849 onwards by the publishing and distribution firm of Smith, Elder & Co. In 1833, the library held approximately 26,000 volumes and considered itself a global institution with a prestige collection worthy of any metropolitan library, aspiring to the status of the Bodleian Library and the Advocate's Library in Edinburgh.[33] This self-perception was augmented in the 1860s by a substantial donation from George Grey (see Chap. 5), which, along with the Dessinian Collection (est. 1761), was thought by the Melbourne *Argus* to elevate the library to 'the position of a first-class library' with a 'collection of books … superior to the collection of any of the second-rate powers in the world, and … in some respects on an equality with such public libraries as are only to be found in London, Paris, and Vienna'.[34] The South African Museum (SAM), incorporated into the same building as the SAPL in 1860, shared its scientific collecting ambitions.[35]

The only other public library of a similar size to the SAPL in the southern colonies was the MPL, which was officially opened to all persons over 14 years of age in 1856. Despite opening with a collection of just 3846 titles, it had universalist ambitions from its inception, and was conceived as a 'national' reference-only collection with a 'noble collection of the best and greatest works in the literature of the world, both ancient and modern'.[36] It also contained an art gallery and museum, with the object of promoting 'sympathy' between 'Literature, Science and Art'.[37] The library received significant support from the state legislature, receiving in 1853 the generous 'sum of three thousand pounds (£3000) for the purchase of books, and ten thousand pounds (£10,000) towards the erection of a suitable building to contain them'. Parliamentary reports indicate that funding for the library remained a priority throughout the 1850s and 1860s, where annual funding for the purchase of books ranged between £2000 and £5000.[38] While the MPL was held up as a model of its kind in America, New Zealand, England, Scotland, and the Australian colonies, and it was claimed that the library ranked 'before a great proportion of similar institutions in Europe' and contained 'more books than any American library, except that at Harvard College', comparisons to major research libraries such as the BML were, for the most part, aspirational.[39] An article in the Melbourne *Herald* in 1862 noted that compared to the 600,000 volumes in the BML, the MPL's 26,000 volumes formed 'but the *basis* of a good provincial library'.[40] By 1870, the MPL contained 57,370 volumes, making it the largest library in colonial Australia in the nineteenth century.

Unlike the MPL, the SAI had its roots in the financial collapse of its most immediate predecessor, the South Australian Library and Mechanics' Institute (SALMI) (est. 1848), itself an amalgamation of the South Australian Literary and Scientific Association (est. 1834) and the Adelaide Mechanics' Institute (est. 1838). Established in 1856, the SAI was a 'Public Library and Museum', as well as featuring an art gallery and a 'School of Art and Design'.[41] The SAI provided a central body to which smaller mechanics' institutes and associations could be either incorporated or affiliated in the manner of the Yorkshire Union of Mechanics' Institutes.[42] Acknowledging that the SAI had at best 'reached mediocrity' by the late 1860s,[43] there was an increasing sense among the colony's elite that the library should abandon its circulating branch and model itself more closely on reference-only libraries, such as the MPL and 'eminent English and American Public Libraries'.[44]

The question of circulation—and the division of a library's circulating and reference branches—was an important one, since, as in British India, many of the most important public libraries in the southern colonies evolved from subscription libraries and mechanics' institutes rather than from centralised municipal legislation, which was enacted in Australia, the Cape Colony, and Singapore in the 1860s and 1870s with mixed results (see Chap. 2). The RLM in Singapore, for example, took over the holdings of the Singapore Library (SL) (1844–1874), a small proprietary subscription library that inherited the holdings of an earlier school library, itself modelled on the Penang Library established in Malacca in 1817.[45] The library was initially housed in the same building as its attached museum, the latter of which grew out of the desire to host permanent colonial exhibitions.[46] The Singapore libraries were supplied by a variety of London agents, libraries, and publishers over time, including Smith, Elder & Co. and Mudie's Circulating Library.

The Sydney FPL likewise had its foundations in a subscription library, the ASL, a substantial proprietary library operating in Sydney from 1826 to 1869 by and for the benefit of an elite membership which jealously guarded its privileges. From 1830 onwards, the ASL's agent in London was James Malcott Richardson, who also supplied the SAPL. Liquidated in 1869, the 16,057 volumes of the ASL were gradually transformed into a substantial reference library over the next 25 years. Unlike many of the public libraries discussed in this book, the ASL was not attached to a museum, and the

Australian Museum, established a year later, was a response to the perceived absence of support for the natural sciences in the Australian colonies.[47] When financial problems resulted in the closure of Hobart's TPL (est. 1849) in its first incarnation, similarly a subscription library for a notably exclusive clientele, the new municipalised TPL was legally constituted through the *Public Libraries Act* of 1867, opening to the public in 1870.[48]

While British library and classificatory models were replicated and transplanted in the Anglosphere colonial world, early public libraries varied considerably across different colonial spaces, with even the Australian colonies—Victoria, Tasmania, South Australia, etc.—having distinct local cultures and place-based identities of their own. Nor did library development always follow a conventional pattern from metropolis to province to colonial outpost, as the extraordinary establishment of a free public library in Cape Town in 1818 suggests. In general, the holdings of these early public libraries were relatively small, with the largest of them holding approximately 30,000–35,000 volumes between 1850 and 1860 and 50,000–60,000 volumes in the 1870s, and the smallest 4000–15,000 between 1850 and 1860 and 3000–20,000 in the 1870s (see Appendix B). This made the smaller libraries, such as the library of the SAI, about the same size as a large mechanics' institute in Leeds or Manchester rather than anything approaching the size of a major research library in Britain or Europe.

But if colonial public libraries had much smaller collections than their British precedents, there was nonetheless an increasing sense among library management committees that they could rival British and European institutions in other ways, particularly in relation to the openness of their institutions, and in the 'civic yield' or use of the libraries per capita.[49] In the chapters that follow, we demonstrate that colonial public libraries increasingly looked to each other—and in particular to the MPL[50]—rather than to the monumental libraries of Britain and Europe as examples of civic modernisation, free and open public access to information, social mobility and egalitarianism, and increased citizenship rights. Even after the British *Public Libraries Acts* of 1850 and 1853, colonial public libraries saw their access policies as improvements on the perceived elitism and closed coteries that persisted in Britain. In this, such libraries were articulating an increasing awareness of their own distinctiveness relating, in part, to their uniquely enhanced geographical distance from the metropolis, but also to evolving cultural attitudes to the relationship between colony, nation, region, and empire.

Notes

1. See, for example, Wallace Kirsop, 'Libraries for an Imperial Power', in *The Cambridge History of Libraries in Britain and Ireland Volume II: 1640–1850*, ed. Giles Mandelbrote and K. A. Manley (Cambridge: Cambridge University Press, 2006), 494–508.
2. The term was used in the nineteenth century to refer to the Cape Colony, New Zealand, and Australia. Kirsten McKenzie, *Scandal in the Colonies: Sydney and Cape Town, 1820–1850* (Melbourne: Melbourne University Press, 2004), 178.
3. See Archie L. Dick, 'Book History, Library History and South Africa's Reading Culture', *South African Historical Journal* 55, no. 1 (2006): 33–45.
4. James Belich, *Replenishing the Earth: The Settler Revolution and the Rise of the Anglo-World, 1783–1939* (Oxford: Oxford University Press, 2009), 5.
5. Isabel Hofmeyr, 'The Globe in the Text: Towards a Transnational History of the Book', *African Studies* 64, no. 1 (2005): 87–103.
6. James Raven, *London Booksellers and their American Customers: Transatlantic Literary Community and the Charleston Library Society, 1748–1811* (Columbia, SC: University of South Carolina Press, 2002), 14.
7. Kyle B. Roberts and Mark Towsey, 'Introduction', in *Before the Public Library: Reading, Community, and Identity in the Atlantic World, 1650–1850*, ed. Kyle B. Roberts and Mark Towsey (Leiden and Boston: Brill, 2018), 1–32 (21).
8. Lynda K. Yankasakas 'Origin Stories: The Boston Athenaeum, Transatlantic Literary Culture, and Regional Rivalry in the Early Republic', *The New England Quarterly* 89, no. 4 (2016): 614–641 (632); Robb. K. Haberman, 'Provincial Nationalism: Civic Rivalry in Postrevolutionary Magazines', *Early American Studies* 10, no. 1 (2012): 162–193. On the intertwined nature of nationalism and globalism, see Benedict Anderson, *Imagined Communities: Reflections on the Origin and Spread of Nationalism* (London: Verso, 1983).
9. Marilyn Lake, 'White Man's Country: The Trans-national History of a National Project', *Australian Historical Studies* 34, no. 122 (2003): 346–363 (348–349).
10. Kathleen Wilson, 'Introduction', in *A New Imperial History: Culture, Identity, and Modernity in Britain and the Empire, 1660–1840*, ed. Kathleen Wilson (New York: Cambridge University Press, 2004), 1–28.
11. Alan Lester, 'Imperial Circuits and Networks: Geographies of the British Empire', *History Compass* 4, no. 1 (2006): 124–141.
12. Gary B. Magee and Andrew S. Thompson, *Empire and Globalisation: Networks of People, Goods and Capital in the British World, c. 1850–1914* (Cambridge: Cambridge University Press, 2010).

13. Tony Ballantyne, *Webs of Empire: Locating New Zealand's Colonial Past* (Vancouver: UBC Press, 2012), 23.
14. Tony Ballantyne, 'Placing Literary Culture: Books and Civic Culture in Milton', *Journal of New Zealand Literature* 28, no. 2 (2010): 82–104 (82).
15. By 1860 the white population of colonial Australia numbered around one million. R. V. Jackson, *Australian Economic Development in the Nineteenth Century* (Canberra: ANU Press, 1977), 4. In contrast, the Aboriginal population had declined rapidly. R. Evans, *A History of Queensland* (Cambridge: Cambridge University Press, 2007), 10–12.
16. By 1860, the total population of Singapore was 90,000, of which only 2445 were Europeans or Eurasians. Saw Swee-Hock, *The Population of Singapore*, 3rd ed. (Singapore: ISEAS Publishing, 2012), 29. In the Cape Colony, the estimated total population in 1865 was 496,381. *Census of the Colony of the Cape of Good Hope, 1865* (Cape Town: Saul Solomon, 1866), iii, viii.
17. David Scott, 'Colonial Governmentality', *Social Text* 43 (1995): 191–220 (204).
18. Julieanne Lamond, 'Communities of Readers: Australian Reading History and Library Loan Records', in *Republics of Letters: Literary Communities in Australia*, ed. Peter Kirkpatrick and Robert Dixon (Sydney: Sydney University Press, 2012), 27–38 (33, 31).
19. Emily B. Todd, 'Antebellum Libraries in Richmond and New Orleans and the Search for the Practices and Preferences of "Real" Readers', *American Studies* 42, no. 3 (2001): 195–209 (196).
20. Wallace Kirsop, 'Writing a History of Nineteenth-Century Commercial Circulating Libraries: Problems and Possibilities', *Bibliographical Society of Australia and New Zealand Bulletin* 27 (2003): 71–82 (80).
21. James Raven, 'Libraries for Sociability: The Advance of the Subscription Library', in *The Cambridge History of Libraries in Britain and Ireland Volume II: 1640–1850*, ed. Giles Mandelbrote and K. A. Manley (Cambridge: Cambridge University Press, 2006), 239–263 (249).
22. Kirsop, 'Libraries for an Imperial Power', 498. Priya Joshi, *In Another Country: Colonialism, Culture, and the English Novel in India* (New York: Columbia University Press, 2002), 63.
23. Leah Price, 'Introduction: Reading Matter', *PMLA* 121, no. 1 (2006): 9–16 (11). Natalie Davies, *Society and Culture in Early Modern France* (Stanford: Stanford University Press, 1975), 192, quoted in Price, 3.
24. Roberts and Towsey, 'Introduction', 19.
25. *Catalogue*, MPL, 1861, v: http://www.ucd.ie/southhem/record.html#112.
26. Both Brunet's *Manuel du Libraire* (1810–1865) and the *Catalogue of the Library of the Royal Institution* (1821) are listed in *Catalogue*, SAPL, 1829: http://www.ucd.ie/southhem/record.html#264.

27. The MPL's 1861 catalogue's alphabetical arrangement with classificatory index often repeats authors across different classifications. We have worked to reduce these repetitions within each of our seven genre categories, but the genre proportions cited should be read as approximate not exact.
28. J. E. Traue, 'The Public Library Explosion in Colonial New Zealand', *Libraries & the Cultural Record* 42, no. 2 (2007): 151–164 (153).
29. Theodorus Friis, *The Public Library in South Africa: An Evaluative Study* (Cape Town: Afrikaanse Pers-Boekhandel 1962), 10.
30. P. R. Coates, 'National Library of South Africa', in *International Dictionary of Library Histories Volumes 1 & 2*, ed. David H. Stam (London and New York: Routledge, 2015), 573–575.
31. *Catalogue*, SAPL, 1844, 2: http://www.ucd.ie/southhem/record.html#460.
32. P. R. Coates, 'Was the South African Library an Athenaeum?', *Quarterly Bulletin of the National Library of South Africa* 66, no. 2 (2012): 11–23 (12).
33. *Catalogue*, SAPL, 1848, 6: http://www.ucd.ie/southhem/record.html#464.
34. *Argus* (Melbourne), March 24, 1862, 6.
35. Saul Dubow, *The Commonwealth of Knowledge: Science, Sensibility, and White South Africa, 1820–2000* (Oxford: Oxford University Press, 2006), 36.
36. *Age* (Melbourne), February 18, 1856, 3.
37. *Report of the Trustees of the Public Library, Museums, and National Gallery of Victoria, with the Reports of the Sectional Committees, for the Year 1870–71* (Melbourne: John Ferres, Government Printer, 1871), accessed August 9, 2018: https://www.parliament.vic.gov.au/vufind/Record/90063.
38. *Catalogue*, MPL, 1861: http://www.ucd.ie/southhem/record.html#112.
39. *Herald* (Melbourne), May 27, 1861, 4. See also the statistical comparisons with the BML in Appendices B and C of the *Report of Trustees, Accompanying Estimates for the Service of the Year 1859* (Melbourne: John Ferres, 1858), 9–10.
40. *Herald*, March 28, 1862, 4.
41. *South Australian Register*, August 22, 1856, 2.
42. Michael Talbot, 'A Close Affiliation: Coordination of Institutes in South Australia', in *Pioneering Culture: Mechanics' Institutes and Schools of Arts in Australia*, ed. Philip C. Candy and John Laurent (Adelaide: Auslib Press, 1994), 335–356. See also *South Australian Register* (Adelaide), August 22, 1856, 2; August 30, 1856, 6.
43. *South Australian Weekly Chronicle* (Adelaide), September 1, 1866, 4.
44. *The South Australian Institute: Comprising the Public Library, Art Gallery, and Museums. Addresses Delivered at the Laying of the Foundation* (Adelaide: W. K. Thomas & Co, 1879), 14.

45. *Singapore Free Press and Mercantile Advertiser*, August 24, 1843, 2; September 21, 1843, 2.
46. *Straits Observer*, May 3, 1875, 21.
47. Matthew Sean Stephens, 'The Australian Museum Library: Its Formation, Function and Scientific Contribution, 1836–1917' (PhD diss., University of New South Wales, 2013), 49–50, accessed February 20, 2019: http://unsworks.unsw.edu.au/fapi/datastream/unsworks:11593/SOURCE1?view=true.
48. John Levett, 'The Tasmanian Free Public Library in 1850: Its Members, Its Managers and its Books', in *Books, Libraries and Readers in Colonial Australia*, ed. Elizabeth Morrison and Michael Talbot (Clayton, Vic: Graduate School of Librarianship, Monash University, 1984), 11–21.
49. Heather Gaunt, 'Identity and Nation in the Australian Public Library: The Development of Local and National Collections 1850s–1940s, Using the Tasmanian Public Library as Case Study' (PhD diss., University of Tasmania, 2010), 152, accessed August 8, 2018: https://eprints.utas.edu.au/10772/. In 1860, the Melbourne *Herald* claimed, for example, that the MPL had a greater annual attendance rate than the BML. *Herald*, May 27, 1861, 4.
50. See, for example, *South Australia Weekly Chronicle*, September 1, 1866, 4; *Queenslander Newspaper*, January 16, 1875, 2.

Open Access This chapter is licensed under the terms of the Creative Commons Attribution 4.0 International License (http://creativecommons.org/licenses/by/4.0/), which permits use, sharing, adaptation, distribution and reproduction in any medium or format, as long as you give appropriate credit to the original author(s) and the source, provide a link to the Creative Commons licence and indicate if changes were made.

The images or other third party material in this chapter are included in the chapter's Creative Commons licence, unless indicated otherwise in a credit line to the material. If material is not included in the chapter's Creative Commons licence and your intended use is not permitted by statutory regulation or exceeds the permitted use, you will need to obtain permission directly from the copyright holder.

CHAPTER 2

From Community to Public Libraries: Liberalism, Education, and Self-Government

Abstract This chapter considers the emergence of public libraries in the southern colonies, looking at how access to knowledge, education, and book provision were understood. It focuses primarily on the various meanings attaching to the word 'public' in the nineteenth century and on the development of 'national' acquisition and collection policies, but it also examines the motivations and catalysts for the development of public libraries more generally, concentrating on the specific, local conditions that led to their establishment and growth, on their connection to political factions concerned with representative government, and on their contribution to a distinctive type of 'colonial modernity'.

Keywords Liberalism • Education • Access • Self-government • Colonial modernity

When, in 1855, *Melbourne Punch* lampooned the soon-to-open MPL for forming a collection of books so valuable and arcane it would seemingly need to be safeguarded from ordinary 'common' readers (Fig. 2.1),[1] the idea of a freely accessible library open to all adult members of the public and paid for by local taxation was still a novel one. Rooted in the principles of self-improvement, rational recreation, and utilitarian thought that underpinned nineteenth-century liberalism, the public library was introduced as a legal entity in Britain and Ireland by the *Public Libraries Acts* of

> **USES OF A PUBLIC LIBRARY.**
>
> I. To be packed in close cases and kept in store for at least a year. This is essential to prevent the books from sustaining the injury which might accrue from exposure on shelves, to the dust of summer or the damp of winter.
>
> II. To be ultimately disposed as far from the centre of population as possible. It is well known that many readers, especially those who have not libraries of their own, and therefore need to use public reading rooms, are very careless of books.
>
> III. Many books which are essential to studious men, contain matter which it is not desirable for various reasons to put into the hands of the general reader. It is therefore highly judicious on the part of the trustees, to obviate this danger by keeping the library out of sight, until they can make arrangements for placing it beyond the reach of the mere lounger.

Fig. 2.1 'Uses of a Public Library', *Melbourne Punch*, August 2, 1855, 153. Courtesy of Trove: https://trove.nla.gov.au/newspaper/article/171430414

1850 and 1853, and the establishment of state-supported free public libraries in the southern colonies was closely associated with this new emblem of 'liberal, democratic citizenship'.[2] Agitating for the establishment of a public library in South Australia, the *Adelaide Observer* pointed out in 1853 that 'the principle of instituting public libraries, supported by taxation is one that is being extensively acted upon in the mother country'.[3] At the inauguration of the new municipal TPL in 1870, the then Governor of Tasmania, Charles Du Cane, made the connection between liberal self-improvement and regional public library provision more explicit when he noted that 'in the great towns of England, no better and easier means of aiding that supplemental self-cultivation has been found than by the establishment of Public Libraries'.[4]

The extent to which the self-improving discourses of nineteenth-century liberalism formed part of a global (and globalising) ideology has been increasingly acknowledged,[5] but contrary to the views of the *Adelaide Observer* the progress of rate-supported municipal libraries in Britain and Ireland was, in fact, slow. By 1868, just 27 local authorities had adopted the public library legislation in Britain; by 1886, the number was 125.[6] The early development of municipal public libraries in the southern colonies was even more protracted. By the 1870s, there was a strong sense that volunteerism had failed in the Straits Settlements, but legislation providing for municipal libraries did not appear until the 1950s.[7] Under legislation enacted between 1869 and 1877, the model promoted and supported by the government in colonial New Zealand remained a user-pays subscription model.[8] In the Cape Colony, the system of government grants established by the *Molteno Regulations* of 1874 slowly but unevenly led to an expansion in the number and size of public libraries.[9] After 1870, the number of municipal public libraries in colonial Australia rose substantially because of legislation such as the New South Wales *Municipalities Act* of 1867 and the Victorian *Education Act* of 1872.[10] By the time of the federation of the Australian colonies in 1901, there were 407 libraries across the nation either fully supported or subsidised by public funds.[11]

Debates over the public function of these and other colonial libraries were primarily articulated through a vigilant local press. In the Cape Colony, the colonial press was critical in giving political shape, and voice, to the dynamic array of propertied settler groups that Kirsten MacKenzie terms the 'colonial public sphere',[12] and the press performed a similar role in the cultural sphere across the southern colonies. Some institutions, such as the SAI, routinely had extensive reports of the proceedings of their general meetings published in the press; others, such as the notoriously elitist ASL, tended to receive press attention only in times of controversy. The press could even play a direct role in facilitating the emergence of some institutions, and the demise of others. The SL, the subscription-based library which replaced the earlier Singapore Institution Library, was established after a lengthy article in the *Singapore Free Press and Mercantile Advertiser* noted 'the want of a really good and proper Public Library' in Singapore, and outlined a plan for such an institution.[13] While colonial newspaper editors frequently had their own political agendas—and newspaper reports about the use and misuse of colonial libraries must therefore be approached with a degree of caution—local newspapers were influential agents in the evolution of colonial public libraries, contributing both to controversies over what manner of institution they were, and what sort of 'public' they should be serving.

LIBERAL VOCABULARIES: THE MEANINGS OF 'PUBLIC' IN THE SOUTHERN COLONIES

During their evolution in the latter half of the nineteenth century, colonial municipal libraries co-existed and sometimes competed with commercial and community libraries with less clear-cut claims to public status. In the Cape Colony and Natal, 39 subscription libraries were established between

1818 and 1873,[14] while in colonial New Zealand, some 263 subscription libraries were founded from 1840 to 1873, and another 506 between 1875 and 1914.[15] In the Straits Settlements, there were little more than a dozen British-run subscription libraries by the mid-nineteenth century.[16] In Australia, circulating and subscription libraries, while plentiful and significant, were gradually supplanted in importance from the 1830s onwards by the libraries attached to mechanics' institutes and related institutions, of which there were nearly 2000 by the end of the century.[17] If these figures are smaller than those of American and British national networks of community libraries,[18] by the end of the century colonial Australia, New Zealand, and South Africa had unprecedentedly high densities of community libraries and mechanics' institutes relative to population.[19]

Prior to the British *Public Libraries Acts*, ideas about what might constitute a public library in the southern colonies varied widely. In the early period of colonisation, the term was often used to describe proprietary libraries which merely inhabited a public space. In 1823, for example, an advertisement was placed in the *Hobart Town Gazette* for a librarian 'competent to conduct a Public Library and Reading Room', adding that if the candidate was 'possessed of sufficient property to take a share in the concern, perhaps it might be more interesting & mutual to both parties'.[20] The subscription library model, dependent as it was on collective middle-class initiative, sociability, and investment,[21] lent itself more easily to the public designation than those purely commercial initiatives run by individual booksellers or auctioneers, since such libraries were often the shared or 'public' property of the denizens of the bourgeois public sphere. When the SAPL was converted from a free library to a subscription library in 1829, for instance, the government announced its decision 'to abandon all claim, interference, and future pecuniary succour to the library, and ... declared it a Public property',[22] reflecting a broader political shift in the Cape Colony towards institutions that served the interests of an increasingly assertive mercantile middle-class elite.[23]

While subscription libraries in the southern colonies have appeared to modern eyes as 'inward-looking, classbound, and isolationist',[24] they can nonetheless be described as 'semi-public' institutions, in that they frequently sought small government grants and/or provided free-to-access reading rooms. As Joanna Innes has succinctly put it, such libraries often felt themselves to have a 'public function' and a 'mission to serve variously conceived publics'.[25] Originally founded to provide educational opportunities to the working classes, mechanics' institutes acted as de facto regional public libraries in colonial Australia and New Zealand. Well before the establishment of the SAI in 1856, the SALMI petitioned the government for a grant for a building, claiming in June 1848 that it was 'a public institution, adapted to the wants of the Colonists, and therefore a public benefit'.[26] In 1865, the *Bendigo Advertiser* noted the close connection between public libraries and those 'kindred institutions' doing public good: 'the Melbourne Public Library … in soliciting for herself [should] not forget that she has morally, if not in law, a family to provide for too'.[27] The SAI was more consciously familial, providing a centralised body to which suburban and regional mechanics' institutes were affiliated, a fact lauded in the Adelaide press with favourable comparisons to the union of mechanics' institutes in Yorkshire.[28]

The sense that private proprietors, subscribers, and donors were 'public benefactors' evincing a 'public spirit' and providing a 'public service' was also evident in the discourses surrounding agitation for the SL and RLM, both of which had relatively inclusive access policies and a variety of subscription rates in order to boost their status as public institutions.[29] In contrast, despite employing a rhetoric of its public significance, the ASL's library committee maintained a deliberately narrow view of the public it was required to serve. When the Colonial Office allowed the sum of £10,000 for the construction of a public library and museum in Sydney (the same amount that would be allowed for the construction of the MPL a decade later), the ASL committee refused to compromise with Governor Sir George Gipps over his requirement to provide a reading room open to the public, opting instead to construct its own privately-funded edifice, at ruinous expense. The New South Wales government would eventually acquire the ASL building and its collection of books at bargain prices for public use as the Sydney FPL.[30]

'Liberality of Access': Reconfiguring Books in the Colonial Public Space

As the controversy over a public reading room at the ASL suggests, debates over the extent to which access to collections should be restricted to subscribers or open to the general public point to the leading role that colonial public libraries played in the 'democratisation of knowledge' that took place throughout the Anglosphere world during the nineteenth century. As Wallace Kirsop has pointed out, the 'push towards greater openness' in the evolution of colonial public libraries 'was not accidental', and was related both to a 'public demand for readier access to books', and to a global network of institutions and settlements that 'stimulated a spirit of emulation'.[31] Debating the admission policies of the SALMI at an annual general meeting in 1848, for example, the question was asked 'whether that Society was for a class, or for the people? Whether it was a Private Society, or a Public Institution?'. Most members agreed that there should be few restrictions to admission, and that 'respectable' men of the 'lower classes' and 'working men' should be admitted to the institution, but concluded that any institution that charged members £1 per annum to access its books could not rightly be called a 'public institution', thereby pointing to free access as a key criterion for a public library.[32]

A second emerging criterion for the status of a public library was that of universal access by all social classes without any forms of recommendation or patronage. The SAPL, for example, was open to all male citizens over the age of 18 from its establishment in 1818. Even after its transition to a subscription-based funding model in the late 1820s, it continued to advertise the availability of its reference collections to 'every class of society': 'no introduction, no recommendation, no securities are required'.[33] Much later in the century, the MPL committee outlined that institution's particularly liberal philosophy, stating in 1861 that it had decided 'to adopt a greater freedom of access and liberality of access to the books than is usual elsewhere' in order to encourage a 'taste for study'.[34] The major concession offered by the MPL, which certainly marked it out from libraries 'elsewhere', was the fact that the library allowed readers unfettered access to its shelves, without any need for a reader's ticket or other form of permission or supervision apart from the signing of a visitor's book.

The liberality of access provided by the SAPL and the MPL was not generally practised in British research libraries during the nineteenth century. As David McVilly notes, visitors to the MPL were 'amazed by the numbers using the library and also by the lack of restrictions placed on them'.[35] Unsupervised public access to shelves was an innovation that remained controversial in Britain for much of the nineteenth century. When Redmond Barry, the guiding figure in the foundation of the MPL and its early development, noted it as an important feature of the institution at the London Congress of Librarians in 1877, the assistant librarian of Cambridge University Library mocked Barry's view that such freedom was 'a right that belonged to the public': 'it was that, in the same sense that it was the idler's right to stroll about for no purpose and doing nothing'.[36] This was not the only aspect of the MPL's liberal admissions policy to attract negative attention from British librarians. At the same conference, Barry was also forced to defend the MPL's policy of admitting readers from the age of 14, somewhat facetiously championing the reading rights of the rising generation by stating that 'if it were necessary to deprive people of seven years' reading, it would be better to strike off the seven years at the other end, and disqualify people at sixty-three'.[37]

While nearly all the early public libraries freely admitted readers to reading rooms after verifying their identity and address, the MPL was unusual in providing extended opening hours from the outset, being open every day except Sunday from 10 am to 10 pm. The SAPL was open for the more modest hours of 10 am to 5 pm in summer and 10 am to 4.30 pm in winter (Sundays and holidays excepted) with limited issuing hours. In 1848, the suggestion of evening opening hours was refused due to a lack of funds.[38] The SL's original opening hours (6 am to 9 pm) reflected the idea that people might come to read after working hours, but by 1849 these hours were reduced from 10.30 am to 5.30 pm.[39] The RLM was similarly open from 10 am to 6 pm except on Sundays.[40] In the 1830s and 1840s, the ASL's subscription-only reading room was open daily (including Sundays) from 10 am to 5 pm, and again from 7 pm to 11 pm. By 1853, it was open from 9 am to 9 pm.[41] When its successor, the FPL, opened in 1869, its equally liberal opening hours were from 10 am to 10 pm.[42] The subscription TPL opened in 1849 with the relatively modest hours of 12 am to 6 pm, gradually increasing its hours in the 1850s.[43] When the TPL opened as a municipal library in 1870, it opened every day from 10 am to 1 pm, 3 pm to 6 pm, and 7 pm until 9 pm, including Sundays.[44] Despite its retention of a membership and subscription fee, the SAI also steadily increased its accessibility over the second half of the century, being open daily (except Sundays) from 12 pm to 10 pm. In 1869, it opened on holiday periods, except Christmas Day and Good Friday. In 1879, it opened on Sundays.[45]

Opening libraries on Sundays and holidays was controversial and often involved arbitrating between secular and religious communities. The former saw the moral and civic benefits of Sunday opening, especially for the working classes who often could not access the library on any other day, and for children between the ages of 12 and 16 (who were usually excluded from early public libraries). Others saw weekend opening hours as contributing to the break-down of domesticity and the nuclear family. As *Melbourne Punch*'s satirical Mrs. Sarah Grundy pointed out in an 1859 article on '"Social Institutions" and "Evils" in General, and "Public Libraries", in Particular', the public library could be a means for avoiding the home as much as it could be a means of edification.[46] For this reason, many public libraries promoted the circulating library as a vital part of their *modus operandi*. In the Cape Colony, for example, the Attorney General William Porter noted the importance of the circulating section of the public library for family reading, a domestic virtue also upheld by the press elsewhere.[47]

While public libraries in the southern colonies generally agreed on the importance of liberal access policies, it was increasingly recognised that the public benefit of free access to books was contingent on the nature of library collections themselves. There was often considerable tension surrounding whether libraries should concentrate on acquiring substantial reference collections, or devote more resources to maintaining collections available for borrowing. Frequently this tension dissolved into familiar arguments over the proportions of 'serious' and 'light' works in the libraries (see Chap. 4), but the sense that a truly 'public' library must account for all types of readers also became a recurring refrain in the southern colonies. As reconceived by Antonio Panizzi during his tenure as Keeper of Printed Books between 1837 and 1856, the BML had attempted to distinguish itself from the 'aristocratic dilettantism' of its original creators by moving to acquire 'common modern books' alongside 'rare, ephemeral, voluminous and costly publications'.[48]

Following Panizzi's distinction between a 'library for education' and a 'library for research', public libraries in the southern colonies were increasingly distinguished from university libraries on the basis both of their rights of access and the kinds of books they stocked. At the laying of the foundation stone of the new South Australian Public Library in 1879, for example, the chairman of the SAI's governing body, Rowland Rees, noted that while the bulk of the library was to 'consist of works of permanent value', the governing body nonetheless proposed 'to provide a library which will meet the requirements of casual readers, as well as those who pursue continuous studies; a place for the deposit of books and the assemblage of readers'.[49] A series of articles in the Melbourne *Herald* in the 1860s and 1870s, on the other hand, condemned the MPL for not stocking popular novels—'Milton, Byron, Tennyson, and Swinburne are admitted: why not also Scott, Dickens, Thackeray, and George Eliot?'—and therefore for not meeting the demands of ordinary readers.[50] For treating books like 'old china', the MPL was accused of being less relevant to the colonial reading public than the 'suburban libraries at Prahran, St Kilda, and Collingwood'.[51]

Legal deposit provisions eventually consolidated the role of public libraries as repositories of all kinds of books, but legal deposit in the colonies did not commence until the 1870s and 1880s, and was not always stringently enforced. In 1866, the *Book Registration Ordinance* in the Straits Settlements required the registration of all books printed in the Straits but did not result in legal deposit. In 1873, the SAPL became the legal deposit library in the Cape Colony. In South Australia and New South Wales, the *Copyright Acts* of 1878 and 1879, respectively, did the same. Despite the 1869 *Copyright Act of Victoria*, it was not until the 1880s that the MPL consolidated its status as a legal deposit library.[52] The strong link in the colonial world between copyright laws and legal deposit suggests that a balance was being sought between the rights of owners, on the one hand, and the users of copyright material, on the other. As the century progressed, this balance was increasingly weighted in favour of the user, promoting the public interest through the encouragement of reading and learning.

A 'HABITAT BUT NO HOME': HOME EDUCATION, SELF-GOVERNMENT, AND INTRA-COLONIAL RIVALRY

Contemporary reflections on reading, books, and libraries are suggestive of their special importance in colonies as far away from Britain as Singapore, South Africa, and Australia. Noting the high level of government support for libraries in British India, the *Singapore Free Press* argued in 1843 that it was important for the 'exiled' Briton with no independent 'home politics' to take up reading: 'to provide against our forming inadequate or false conceptions of what takes place at a distance it is clearly necessary that we should have access to books'.[53] While a fear of 'false conceptions' partly explains the colonial desire to 'keep up-to-date' with the latest print and news, and to be 'almost on par with those at home as regards the literature and science of the passing day',[54] an emerging awareness of the heightened moral importance of reading in the colonies appears in New Zealand Company propaganda in 1833:

> none but they who have resided in a new colony can appreciate the value of a new book; and we are happy to bear testimony, that in no colony is literature more appreciated than in New Zealand: as might be expected from the very superior class of men who have migrated to our favourite colony.

If part of this propaganda was to distinguish the free New Zealand settlements from the penal colonies of New South Wales, Van Diemen's Land, and Singapore, there was nonetheless a prevailing sense among colonial communities that good reading encouraged civility: 'a well-conducted colonist is of necessity a reading man'.[55]

Fear of the effects of isolation and distance from metropolitan seats of knowledge took on a particular importance in the tropical climates of Singapore, Penang, and Malacca, where reading was seen as a counter to fears about physical, mental, and moral degeneration in the tropics, as well as to fears about miscegenation and proximity to 'native' populations.[56] Comparable arguments about distance, degeneration, and the curative role of reading were also made in relation to those 'wayward' young men that settler colonies were perceived to attract in great numbers. The physician and future Chairman of the RLM committee, Robert Little, argued that a public library in Singapore would be one 'of the greatest safeguards we could find for the young people of the Settlement': 'being able to read an entertaining novel, a well written history, "or an instructive biography," might keep them at home at night and save them from the gaming table'. While the *Straits Observer* scoffed at Little's claims that a public library could convince young men to 'stop home like good boys',[57] a similar argument about the need to safeguard the youth of the colony was made in the Cape Colony, with numerous commentators noting the importance of shaping the taste of the young men on whom 'the hope of the Colony' depended.

In 1848, the Chief Justice of the Cape Colony, Sir John Wylde, noted a shift in the demographics of the SAPL's users, facilitated by a new, cheaper subscription rate, from old gentlemen to young professionals. The new subscribers were 'for the most part, young men in public service—or, in attorneys' offices—, or in merchants' counting-houses', in other words, the future administrators of the colony 'advancing to take our places'.[58] By including lower-middle-class professionals within the library's remit, and investing in them the virtues of 'serious' reading, the SAPL sought to play a central role in shaping the moral and intellectual life of the Cape Colony's future leaders. In 1853, W. A. Newman, the first Dean of Cape Town, likewise stressed the moral role a public library could have in the lives of young colonists far from their places of birth. In referring to these young men of the Cape as having a 'habitat but no home', Newman was referencing the terms of the 1818 proclamation establishing the SAPL, which claimed the purpose of the library was 'to lay the foundation of a system which shall place the means of Knowledge within the reach of the youth of this Colony, and bring within their reach what the most eloquent of ancient writers has considered to be one of the first blessings of life—HOME EDUCATION'.[59]

While Newman does not draw any explicit connections between home education and home rule, other commentary about the SAPL in the lead-up to the establishment of representative government (est. 1853) suggests how closely the rhetoric surrounding education was linked to questions of self-governance. In his 1848 speech to SAPL subscribers, James Adamson, Professor of English and Classics at the South African College (est. 1829), made clear the strong link between thriving educational institutions and colonial self-determination:

> I feel satisfied that we could have in this colony all the means of educating our youth for every one of the learned professions, if only we set our heart and hand. Unless we do so, we can never flourish as a community,—for without education we are as naught; we act not upon those liberal principles that tend to the advancement of society … and direct us in the road to that future which we hope to attain.[60]

Adamson's sense of the SAPL as a decisive intervention into the colony's progress towards emerging nation-statehood came increasingly to the fore in 1853. In that year, Governor Harry Smith called for improved education provision at the Cape, citing Nova Scotia as an example of the benefits of universal education and linking the importance of 'serious reading' with the establishment of a legislative assembly. The nation's future law givers, Smith implied, had a moral and civic responsibility to be well cultivated; intellectual seriousness was essential for the colony to be taken seriously as a semi-autonomous nation.[61]

In Victoria, too, the MPL was linked to questions of self-government and the assertion of an independent local identity. The library was one of several rapidly-formed institutions after the separation of the colony of Victoria from New South Wales in 1850, including a new Supreme Court (est. 1853), the University of Melbourne (est. 1853), and Legislative Chambers (est. 1856).[62] Seeing the MPL as part of a 'cluster' of institutions intended to support the colony's learning, culture, and independence helps us to better understand its significance as an institution intertwined with aspects of colonial self-determination and nation-building. If by 1860 the Cape Colony, New Zealand, and all of the Australian colonies, apart from Western Australia, had been granted either representative or responsible self-government and had their own legislative assemblies, the establishment of a functioning public library was nonetheless acknowledged to be part of a process of intellectual and civic maturity leading up to more decisive acts of self-determination such as Australian Federation and responsible government in the Cape—acts that were entangled with questions of intra-colonial rivalry and the issue of relative status within imperial hierarchies.[63]

These rivalries suggest both an awareness of a colony's status within a wider British Empire and more ambitious assertions of colonial intellectual accomplishment. Complaining in 1854 about the lack of public lectures at the SAI, the *South Australian Register* displayed a keen awareness of developments both inside and outside the Australian colonies: 'for a long time we have been greatly outdone in these matters by the neighbouring colonies of Victoria, New South Wales, and Tasmania. In England … the leading in the State … assert the highest places in the temples of literature and science'.[64] Four years later, a letter to the editor in the same newspaper noted the SAI's lack of display space, arguing that the government needed to provide 'more suitable accommodation for books and readers' because 'doubtless this is often referred to with a sneer by our more influential neighbours. We receive specimens from the Cape, from Victoria, from various parts of our own colony, but have no eligible place to house them'.[65]

The SAPL committee similarly argued in 1857 that it was 'not too soon for South Africa' to follow the examples of New South Wales and Canada in establishing public institutions 'when intelligence and commercial prosperity in this colony bid fair to rival an attainment exemplified in the older countries', signalling an intention not just to replicate British institutions but to outdo them.[66] As early as 1853, Governor Smith went as far as to describe the SAPL as the preeminent public library in the British world, arguing that in Britain itself there was only one truly public library, Chetham's Library in Manchester, which had only 20,000 volumes to the SAPL's 32,000.[67] Smith's hyperbole aside, it was acknowledged in Britain both that the state of those libraries open to the general public had fallen behind similar libraries in Europe and America, and that they were inaccessible to the working classes.[68] It was also recognised that the SAPL 'would stand a comparison with almost any library in England, the national ones excepted'.[69] The MPL, too, was declared a rival to many of the libraries in the Anglophone world, suggesting the extent to which colonial libraries measured their success on a global scale. As one correspondent to the Melbourne *Argus* confidently claimed: 'as to the United States libraries, I shall be no less gratified than surprised if, on visiting any one of them, I find in it a collection of books equally valuable with that which Melbourne already boasts, and at the same time equally free from chaff'.[70]

'Hardly its Equal in Point of Beauty and Convenience': Colonial Public Libraries as Agencies of Modernity

Smith's claim in 1853 that the SAPL was the largest truly public library in the British world reflected the growing sense in both Britain and its colonies that the large research libraries of Britain and continental Europe were only nominally 'public'. As one correspondent to the London *Times* pointed out in 1841, the BML, with its specialised collections, restricted opening hours and admission policies, and small number of users, was 'a mere sealed book to the million'.[71] Even after 1850, when the BML was legally a public library, admission still required a letter of recommendation and a reading card.[72] Despite modelling itself on the BML, the MPL, with its liberal access policies designed to promote a freer scholarly environment, saw itself working 'against the inroads of that exclusive spirit which has so greatly diminished the usefulness of similar establishments in England'.[73]

While the size of the collections of colonial libraries remained well below those of major British and European libraries, Smith was right to point out that colonial libraries could outstrip metropolitan libraries in terms of rights of access, facilities, and modern technologies. The MPL and the SAI, for example, both enjoyed gas lighting by the 1860s—a full two decades before the BML—and despite its troubled financial circumstances, the ASL also had gas lighting installed in its building from its opening in 1845.[74] Ventilation in the MPL was technologically advanced, including 'flues carried through the main walls' and 'air tubes leading … to the roof'.[75] In a letter to his London bookseller, J. J. Guillaume, Redmond Barry was confident that the books in the MPL enjoyed better conditions than those in libraries in London: 'here we enjoy perfect ventilation and absolute freedom from damp, smoke, soot, or the disagreeable atmospheric and climactic annoyances of which in England complaint is made. Gas hitherto has not produced the deleterious effects which have been so destructive in the Athenaeum Library and elsewhere in Europe'.[76] While Barry's optimism regarding the effect of gas on the books in the MPL proved misplaced, his belief that its reading room had 'hardly its equal in point of beauty and convenience either on the European continent or in England' was more well founded. Far from being a poor copy of metropolitan institutions, the reading room was both beautiful and practical, being able to seat up to 650 people, whereas the BML's reading room could seat 450 people in 1861 and in 1862 was reduced to 350 per day.[77]

The accelerated modernity of colonial libraries was self-consciously cultivated by nineteenth-century library committees, who not only saw the public library as a symbol of the social mobility and democratic potential of colonial societies, but also as a microcosm of the remarkably intense condensation of the various stages of capitalism and social development that took place in the colonial world. In his address at the opening of the Ballarat Free Public Library in 1869, Barry dismissed the idea that 'Australia has no history', arguing that the inhabitants of Australia had instead bypassed the infant stages of society and 'come into the possession of our estate in the full vigor of matured manhood'.[78] The ability of colonial societies to skip stages of social development and transform themselves into modern societies was aided by the population explosion occasioned by the gold rushes in Australia and New Zealand in the 1850s and 1860s. The total population of all the Australian colonies increased almost fourfold from 430,000 in 1851 to 1.7 million in 1871, one of the most prominent examples of what James Belich has identified as a series of 'settlement booms' associated with Anglophone expansion throughout the nineteenth century.[79] Such 'booms' were accompanied by rapid commercial, industrial, and technological development, which enabled an equally rapid development in social and cultural institutions.[80]

At the same time, public and other institutional libraries were positioned as antidotes to the greed of gold rushes and the mercantile nature of colonial societies more generally. An article in the *Straits Times* in 1846 argued for the need for a public library in Singapore because the settlement was almost 'exclusively mercantile' and 'fully a century behind other settlements' in its cultural development.[81] David Goodman has argued that libraries and other cultural institutions were similarly 'central to the attempt by elites to reassert order in gold-rush Victoria', where they helped to combat the perceived social malaise symbolised above all by the unsettled, migratory life of the digger.[82] The grandeur of the MPL, the eminently scholarly nature of its collections, and its prestigious first major catalogue of 1861 provided a highly visible redress to the idea that colonial life was purely self-interested and materialistic.[83] Similarly, the *South Australian Weekly Chronicle* referred in 1866 to the importance of the SAI's role in 'cultivating the public taste'.[84]

Colonial public libraries were therefore perceived to be agencies of modernity at the frontier of colonial taste-formation and civic modernisation, both in a material and intellectual sense. This new kind of 'colonial modernity' was self-consciously distinctive from metropolitan modernity, not only temporally and spatially but also in its attention to a peculiarly colonial egalitarianism and inventiveness. The committee of the MPL argued, for example, that whereas in England university education 'has tended most banefully' towards 'mere learned accomplishments', the libraries and universities of the colonial world had the opportunity to encourage invention and creativity.[85] A letter to the Melbourne *Argus* in 1856 entitled 'Books within reach of our "Inventors"' agreed with the MPL committee, noting the use made of available scientific books and periodicals by enterprising patrons.[86] In 1879, the Governor of South Australia went further in maintaining that a library and museum for the masses should have a technological and industrial department along the lines of the Museum of Industry in Dublin, the Imperial Technical School in Moscow, and the School of Practical Science in Toronto. If his argument was qualified by the claim that 'in an industrial country like South Australia the utilitarian must take priority of the aesthetical'—at least until such time as art could 'take the place in the life of this colony that it has occupied in the past history of older countries, and that it occupies even now in the adjoining province of Victoria'— there was nonetheless a sense that in the southern colonies 'inventive genius' was, or could be, 'ever active'.[87]

BUILDING THE NATIONAL COLLECTION: PUBLIC MONUMENTS AND LOCAL ARCHIVES

While the collections of colonial public libraries provided unique opportunities for both intellectual innovation and a colony's self-promotion, library buildings were among the most important material signifiers of their cultural ambitions. Nearly all of the purpose-built 'landmark' premises housing these major colonial libraries were neo-classical in style, emphasising the importance of the library as a display of cultural capital, as well as being a marker of respectability, and of 'civic identity and proper civic behaviour'.[88] As the trustees of the SAI remarked in their third annual report, a landmark building would be 'the means by which the Institute will be enabled to step forth from its present character of a mere circulating library on a somewhat liberal footing, and enter on the career of public utility marked out for it by the Legislature'.[89] For this reason, debates about where and how a 'central' and 'national' public library should be built were fierce.[90]

Many of the buildings were modelled on existing buildings in Britain. The SAPL building inaugurated in late 1860, for example, was based on George Basevi's 1845 design for the Fitzwilliam Museum in Cambridge,

Fig. 2.2 Samuel Calvert, 'The Reading Room of the Melbourne Public Library', wood engraving, *Illustrated Melbourne Post*, June 27, 1866. Courtesy of the State Library of Victoria: http://handle.slv.vic.gov.au/10381/295506

while the MPL and RLM buildings were neo-Palladian in style. The internal spaces of colonial libraries did not, however, tend to mirror the 'panoptic character' of the BML reading room, with its central structure housing the library's staff.[91] Instead, gallery-style reading rooms, such as those in the SAI and the MPL, either provided free public access to shelves or allowed books to be visible to the user, reflecting new democratic models of self-surveillance (Fig. 2.2).[92]

That the rotundas, porticos, pantheons, colonnades, and Corinthian columns of these neo-classical structures were meant to symbolise a connection to 'time-honoured cultural values' was made explicit by Redmond Barry when he delivered a lecture to the workmen employed in building the Rotunda and Great Hall of the MPL for the Intercolonial Exhibition of 1866. Beginning with a brief history of architecture, ancient and modern, Barry provided a detailed comparative analysis of the scale of the MPL in relation to other important buildings across time and space: 'it is 220 feet long, 82 wide, so that, with the exception of those of Padua, Ypres, and our own Westminster, there is none in Europe enumerated above which exceeds it in length, while it is larger than four of England's cathedrals'.[93] As these comments suggest, colonial public libraries sought both to harness and to rival the prestige of major institutions abroad, creating 'statements to posterity' associated with rising proto-national sentiments, while also championing a new spirit of democratic openness that challenged the perceived elitism of British metropolitan institutions.[94] Although colonial public libraries were clearly modelled on British institutions and designed to show allegiance to imperial institutions and ideologies, they were also often equally carefully organised to emphasise national and regional affiliations.

One means of foregrounding nascent 'national' intellectual accomplishment was in the archiving of scholarly material relating to the colonies, and the collection of local print culture more generally. The SAPL was perhaps the most advanced in this regard. Its chief librarian from 1828 to 1844, Alexander Jardine, was an active collector of books in all genres (but especially voyages and travels) about the Cape, and he also collected and archived the products of the Cape presses. In the 1829 SAPL catalogue, there are eight volumes of works from the Cape presses listed, including pamphlets, reports, essays, correspondence, and ordinances, as well as three volumes of papers 'relating to the Cape of Good Hope'.[95] By 1842, works printed by the Cape presses include 17 volumes of pamphlets on various topics (written in English and Dutch), as well as copies of all the Cape newspapers and periodicals.[96] The 1862 catalogue is also notable for being the first to have a classificatory category specifically devoted to books about and from South Africa, as well as including for the first time George Grey's ethnological and philological collections.[97]

Acknowledging the importance of collectors such as Grey, colonial library committees were increasingly aware of their role as archivists of regional knowledge as the nineteenth century progressed, particularly in the fields of philology, ethnography, and natural history (see Chap. 5). The *Straits Times* argued in 1846 for the importance of studying the antiquities, ethnography, and various tribes of the Malay Archipelago, suggesting that the association of a Literary and Scientific Institution with the library would render it 'more efficient and useful'.[98] Such an institution, the Straits

Branch of the Royal Asiatic Society, was eventually established in 1877, an event which coincided with a new catalogue of the RLM with classifications devoted to the philology and ethnography of the Malay Archipelago, as well as to books about and from the Malay world. The 1877 catalogue lists, for example, thirty books under the new classificatory category 'Eastern Archipelago & Straits Settlements'.[99]

Heather Gaunt has shown that public libraries in colonial Australia, on the other hand, and in contrast to British regional equivalents, were haphazard in their collection of local material.[100] While the trustees of the SAI noted at their annual general meeting in 1861 that 'it has always appeared to the Board to be almost a matter of public duty that each of the Australian colonies should possess works so peculiarly devoted to them',[101] the percentage of local material in colonial libraries was often small. The 1848/1849 catalogue of the SALMI, for example, contains Charles Sturt's *Expeditions in Australia* (1849) and a small number of texts on various Australian colonies and provinces in its 'Topography and Travels' section, but the library was not seriously collecting local works at this time. By 1869, its predecessor, the SAI, had a larger proportion of works on the Australian colonies and surrounding regions, as well as a full collection of state papers for the Australian and New Zealand colonies, but its Australiana collection could by no means be considered substantial.[102]

Local collections at the ASL/FPL, MPL, and TPL were similarly limited. The TPL did not substantially develop its Australiana collection until the 1920s and 1930s.[103] Similarly, the ASL did not collect the productions of the local press, arguing that they were 'neither extensive, expensive nor difficult to obtain'. Its archival function was nonetheless serendipitously amplified by a bequest of nearly 1000 volumes of books, manuscripts, pamphlets, and newspapers from Edward Wise in 1865, as well as by the FPL's librarian R. C. Walker's interest in increasing the library's Australiana holdings from the 1870s onwards.[104] By the 1890s, the (then) Public Library of New South Wales, under the librarianship of H. C. L. Anderson, had a much more substantial Australasian collection but it was once again significantly bolstered by a magnificent bequest of some 60,000 volumes of early Australian books, pamphlets, and manuscripts, as well as works relating to the Pacific, East Indies, and Antarctica, from David Scott Mitchell in 1907.[105]

For public libraries such as the FPL and the MPL, neglecting local material could be controversial. Even before the period in the late-nineteenth century when 'colonial editions' were aggressively marketed to colonial audiences by the metropolitan book trade,[106] the MPL had to repeatedly defend itself against accusations that it was not archiving local and regional colonial productions or supporting the local print industry. According to Charles Gavan Duffy (later a trustee of the library), the MPL contained 'not a single volume on Australian affairs' when it opened to the public in 1856. Duffy accordingly considered the MPL 'strangely unfit for its position in the capital of a new country'.[107] The Melbourne press tended to concur, with the library gaining a reputation in the 1860s and 1870s for acquiring British and European material at the expense of more local and regional material. In 1874, the *Herald* criticised the library for dedicating too much space to unread and out-of-place classics, citing an Italian edition of Bocaccio, while 'matters relating to Australia are too much ignored'. A few years later, the *Austral Review* similarly called on the MPL to 'let the Greek Dryasdusts stifle, but not our Australian youth anxious for knowledge of their native land'. By 1879, the Melbourne *Age* claimed that 'the colonial department is notoriously incomplete and that of our own colony ... the most meagre'.[108]

Although Redmond Barry was indeed concerned to build the library's reputation in certain prestige areas such as Greek and Latin, Shakespeariana, and editions and translations of the Bible, these charges were not entirely fair. McVilly notes that up until 1869, when the MPL received legal deposit rights, it 'purchased most of the serious works published in Victoria, while not going out of its way to chase fugitive material', as well as purchasing books published in England about the Australian colonies. Even if it was less interested in material emanating from other colonies, the MPL did collect printed works on South Asia from several sources from 1853 to 1880, including from Frederik Muller in Amsterdam and from large London booksellers such as James Bain, Bernard Quaritch, and Henry Sotheran. While acquisitions on British India tended to be based on classical or Orientalist foundations, the collection also included dictionaries, grammars, and readers in modern Indian languages, travels and voyages to India, contemporary periodicals such as the *Calcutta Review*, and Indian tracts and pamphlets, primarily on modern Indian politics.[109] Moreover, exchanges of volumes, pamphlets, and maps from India occurred on a large scale from 1870 onwards.[110]

After the MPL's early collection was formed largely through Barry's dealings with the London bookseller Guillaume and other overseas booksellers, a letter to the editor of the *Herald* newspaper in 1861 asked why 'the grants of money voted to the public library are not expended in this country', and promoted the booksellers of Melbourne as having 'some of the rarest and best known works, as well as the more modern, and good supplies of those just published'.[111] Although the MPL was defended by, among others, the Melbourne bookseller H. T. Dwight, who claimed he had a '"standing order" from the trustees to supply the library with all colonial publications', and the library did indeed purchase books from local booksellers as well as at auctions and from private collections,[112] critics remained unconvinced by the MPL's support of a nascent Australian print and publishing culture. By the 1880s, ongoing complaints resulted in all non-British periodical publications being purchased through local booksellers, and, after Barry's death, the trustees of the MPL cancelled all standing orders with overseas firms, dramatically reducing European purchases in favour of Melbourne purchases.[113]

While those advocating for public libraries in the southern colonies drew on the globalising rhetoric of liberal metropolitan discourses relating to universal education and self-improvement, they were also driven by particular local or regional imperatives such as the acquisition of local books, the archiving of regional knowledge, and the production of ethnographic field work, as well as by more local questions surrounding colonial self-determination and independence. The importance of studying and collecting local natural history, ethnography, and antiquities, the vast distances from metropolitan cultural institutions and seats of knowledge, the need to educate both British emigrant and Indigenous populations, the perceived dangers of living in the tropics, and the special problems of itinerant diggers and 'wayward youths'—these were all causes for comment and concern in public discourse, and problems for which colonial public libraries were looked to as a potential remedy. In this way, colonial public libraries were both embedded in their local surroundings and formed part of a wider culture of nineteenth-century liberalism in Britain, Europe, and North America, to which they both reacted and contributed.

NOTES

1. 'Uses of a Public Library', *Melbourne Punch*, August 2, 1855, 153.
2. Patrick Joyce, 'The Politics of the Liberal Archive', *History of the Human Sciences* 12, no. 2 (1999): 35–49 (35).
3. *Adelaide Observer*, Supplement, December 3, 1853, 1.
4. Quoted in Heather Gaunt, 'Identity and Nation in the Australian Public Library: The Development of Local and National Collections 1850s–1940s, Using the Tasmanian Public Library as Case Study' (PhD diss., University of Tasmania, 2010), 54, accessed August 8, 2018: https://eprints.utas.edu.au/10772/.

5. See, for example, Regenia Gagnier, *Individualism, Decadence and Globalization. On the Relationship of Part to Whole, 1859–1920* (Basingstoke: Palgrave Macmillan, 2010).
6. Alistair Black, 'The People's University', in *The Cambridge History of Libraries in Great Britain and Ireland Volume III 1850–2000*, ed. Alistair Black and Peter Hoare (Cambridge: Cambridge University Press, 2006), 24–39 (27).
7. *Straits Times Overland Journal* (Singapore), December 31, 1874, 3. Edward Lim Huck Tee, *Libraries in West Malaysia and Singapore* (Kuala Lumpur: University of Malaya Library, 1970), 36.
8. J. E. Traue, 'The Public Library Explosion in Colonial New Zealand', *Libraries and the Cultural Record* 42, no. 2 (2007): 151–164 (153).
9. Theodorus Friis, *The Public Library in South Africa: An Evaluative Study* (Cape Town: Afrikaanse Pers-Boekhandel, 1962), 69.
10. David J. Jones, 'Public Library Development in New South Wales', *The Australian Library Journal* 54, no. 2 (2003): 130–137.
11. Peter Biskup and Doreen Goodman, *Australian Libraries*, 3rd ed. (London: Clive Bingley, 1982), 81.
12. Kirsten McKenzie, '"Franklins of the Cape": The *South African Commercial Advertiser* and the Creation of a Colonial Public Sphere, 1824–1854', *Kronos* 25 (1998/1999): 88–102.
13. *Singapore Free Press and Mercantile Advertiser*, September 21, 1843, 2. R. Hantisch, 'Raffles Library and Museum, Singapore', in *One Hundred Years of Singapore*, ed. Walter Makepeave, Gilbert Brook, and Roland Braddell, 2 vols (London: John Murray, 1921), 1: 519–566 (526).
14. Jacqueline Audrey Kalley, 'The Effect of Apartheid on the Provision of Public, Provincial and Community Library Services in South Africa with Particular Reference to the Transvaal' (PhD Diss., University of Natal, 1994), 15.
15. Traue, 'The Public Library Explosion', 152.
16. Tee, *Libraries in West Malaysia*, 11–15.
17. Derek A. Whitelock, *The Great Tradition: A History of Adult Education in Australia* (St Lucia, Qld: University of Queensland Press, 1974), 127. Philip Candy, '"The Light of Heaven Itself": The Contribution of the Institutes to Australia's Cultural History', in *Pioneering Culture: Mechanics Institutes and Schools of Art in Australia*, ed. P. C. Candy and J. Laurent (Adelaide: Auslib Press, 1994), 1–28 (2).
18. For US statistics, see Wayne A. Wiegand, *Part of our Lives: A People's History of the American Public Library* (Oxford: Oxford University Press, 2015), 12, 48–49.
19. Traue, 'The Public Library Explosion', 158.
20. *Hobart Town Gazette*, February 15, 1823, 2.

21. James Raven, 'The Advance of the Subscription Library', in *Cambridge History of Libraries in Britain and Ireland Volume II 1640–1850*, ed. Giles Mandelbrote and K. A. Manley (Cambridge: Cambridge University Press, 2006), 239–263.
22. *Catalogue*, SAPL, 1831, 8: http://www.ucd.ie/southhem/record.html#265.
23. Saul Dubow, *The Commonwealth of Knowledge: Science, Sensibility, and White South Africa, 1820–2000* (Oxford: Oxford University Press, 2006).
24. John Levett, 'The Tasmanian Public Library 1849–1869: The Rise and Fall of a Colonial Institution' (Masters Thesis, Monash University, 1984), 79.
25. Joanna Innes, 'Libraries in Context; Social, Cultural and Intellectual Background', in *Cambridge History of Libraries in Britain and Ireland Volume II 1640–1850*, ed. Giles Mandelbrote and K. A. Manley (Cambridge: Cambridge University Press, 2006), 285–300 (285).
26. *South Australian Register* (Adelaide), June 20, 1848, 2.
27. *Bendigo Advertiser*, January 10, 1865, 2.
28. *South Australian Register*, August 22, 1856, 2. See also *South Australian Register*, August 30, 1856, 6.
29. *Singapore Free Press and Mercantile Advertiser*, September 21, 1843, 2.
30. F. M. Bladen, *Public Library of New South Wales: Historical Notes*, 2nd ed. (Sydney: Govt. Printer, 1911), esp. 8–41.
31. Wallace Kirsop, 'Libraries for an Imperial Power', in *Cambridge History of Libraries in Britain and Ireland Volume II 1640–1850*, ed. Giles Mandelbrote and K. A. Manley (Cambridge: Cambridge University Press, 2006), 494–508 (496–97).
32. *South Australian Register*, November 29, 1848, 2. See also *Adelaide Times*, September 13, 1851, 5.
33. *Catalogue*, SAPL, 1842, v: http://www.ucd.ie/southhem/record.html#269.
34. *Catalogue*, MPL, 1861, vi: http://www.ucd.ie/southhem/record.html#112.
35. David McVilly, '"Something to Blow About"?—the State Library of Victoria, 1856–1880', *La Trobe Journal* 8 (1971): 81–90 (82).
36. Quoted in Wallace Kirsop, 'Redmond Barry and the Libraries', *La Trobe Journal* 73 (2004): 55–66 (64–65).
37. Kirsop, 'Redmond Barry and the Libraries', 65.
38. *Catalogue*, SAPL, 1829: http://www.ucd.ie/southhem/record.html#264; *Catalogue*, SAPL, 1831: http://www.ucd.ie/southhem/record.html#265; *Catalogue*, SAPl, 1837: http://www.ucd.ie/southhem/record.html#268; *Catalogue*, SAPL, 1848: http://www.ucd.ie/southhem/record.html#464.
39. *Singapore Library Report 1845*, 6–7.

40. *Straits Observer* (Singapore), May 3, 1875, 21. *Straits Settlements Annual Reports for the Year 1874* (Singapore: Government Printing Office 1875), 121–122.
41. *Catalogue*, ASL, 1839, 22: http://www.ucd.ie/southhem/record.html#30; *Catalogue*, ASL, 1843, 24: http://www.ucd.ie/southhem/record.html#33; *Catalogue*, ASL, 1853, n.p.: http://www.ucd.ie/southhem/record.html#520.
42. *Sydney Morning Herald*, May 26, 1871, 5.
43. *Catalogue*, TPL, 1849, vi: http://www.ucd.ie/southhem/record.html#480; *Catalogue*, TPL, 1852, ix: http://www.ucd.ie/southhem/record.html#327; *Catalogue* TPL, 1855, xi: http://www.ucd.ie/southhem/record.html#312; *Catalogue*, TPL, 1862, 11: http://www.ucd.ie/southhem/record.html#482.
44. *Catalogue*, TPL, 1871, 6: https://trove.nla.gov.au/goto?i=x&w=35488264&d=http%3A%2F%2Fhandle.slv.vic.gov.au%2F10381%2F200582&s=fMgPfYTpRceruXgIT1Goh01SWTRn7GoW1mLBl9P3UCQ%3D.
45. *Adelaide Observer*, September 27, 1856, 1. *South Australian Register*, November 29, 1848, 2; October 13, 1869, 2.
46. *Melbourne Punch*, July 14, 1859, 3.
47. *Catalogue*, SAPL, 1848, 13: http://www.ucd.ie/southhem/record.html#464.
48. Marvin Spevack, 'The Impact of the British Museum Library', in *Cambridge History of Libraries in Britain and Ireland Volume II 1640–1850*, ed. Giles Mandelbrote and K. A. Manley (Cambridge: Cambridge University Press, 2006), 422–437 (435).
49. *The South Australian Institute: Comprising the Public Library, Art Gallery, and Museums. Addresses Delivered at the Laying of the Foundation Stone* (Adelaide: W. K. Thomas, 1879), 8.
50. *Herald* (Melbourne), September 20, 1874, 2. See also *Herald*, March 28, 1862, 4.
51. *Herald*, December 5, 1876, 2.
52. Elizabeth Morrison, 'The Archaeology of Australian Colonial Newspapers', in *Australian Serials: Current Developments in Bibliography*, ed. Carol Mills and John Mills (New York: Haworth Press, 1991), 35–51 (46); R. C. Barrington Partridge, *The History of the Legal Deposit of Books Throughout the British Empire* (London: Library Association, 1938), 157–167.
53. *Singapore Free Press and Mercantile Advertiser*, August 24, 1843, 2.
54. C. B. Buckley, *An Anecdotal History of Old Times in Singapore*, 2 vols (Singapore: Fraser and Neave, 1902), 1: 442.
55. *New Zealand Journal*, July 13, 1844, quoted in Traue, 'The Public Library Explosion', 159.

56. *Singapore Library Report 1849* (Singapore: G. M. Frederick at the Singapore Press Office, 1849), 9. See also Brendan Luyt, 'Centres of Calculation and Unruly Colonists: The Colonial Library in Singapore and its Users, 1874–1900', *Journal of Documentation* 64, no. 3 (2008): 386–396 (390).
57. *Straits Observer*, December 28, 1874, 2.
58. *Catalogue*, SAPL, 1848, 13: http://www.ucd.ie/southhem/record.html#464.
59. *Catalogue*, SAPL, 1842, iii: http://www.ucd.ie/southhem/record.html#269. On the affective meanings of 'home', see Jason R. Rudy, *Imagined Homelands: British Poetry in the Colonies* (Baltimore: Johns Hopkins University Press, 2017), 6.
60. *Catalogue*, SAPL, 1848, 7–8: http://www.ucd.ie/southhem/record.html#464.
61. *Catalogue*, SAPL, 1853, 8–17: http://www.ucd.ie/southhem/record.html#469.
62. Sue Reynolds, 'Libraries, Librarians, and Librarianship in the Colony of Victoria', *Australian Academic and Research Libraries* 40, no. 1 (2013): 50–64 (59).
63. See Redmond Barry's connection between public libraries and a 'confederating' sentiment in his *Address on the Opening of The Free Public Library of Ballarat East by Sir Redmond Barry* (Ballarat: The Star Office, 1869), 5, 6, 22.
64. *South Australian Register*, August 12, 1854, 3.
65. *South Australian Register*, April 20, 1858, 3.
66. *Catalogue*, SAPL, 1857, 5: http://www.ucd.ie/southhem/record.html#471.
67. *Catalogue*, SAPL, 1853, 19: http://www.ucd.ie/southhem/record.html#469. For contemporary complaints about Chetham's access hours, see Edwin Waugh, *Lancashire Sketches* (Frankfurt Am Main: Outlook Verlag, 2018), 222.
68. Lewis C. Roberts, 'Disciplining and Disinfecting Working-Class Readers in the Victorian Public Library', *Victorian Literature and Culture* 26, no. 1 (1998): 105–132 (106).
69. 'Cape of Good Hope Public Library', *Mechanics' Magazine, Museum, Register, Journal and Gazette* 25 (1836): 222–223 (222). Robert Montgomery Martin, *History of the Colonial Library, Vol. 3: History of South Africa* (London: Whitaker & Co., 1836), 207.
70. *Argus* (Melbourne), January 2, 1860, 6.
71. *Times* (London), October 16, 1841, 5.
72. Joyce, 'Politics of the Liberal Archive', 41.
73. *Argus*, July 6, 1855, 5.

74. ASL, *Minutes and Proceedings, 1826–1846*, October 12, 1829, *Australian Library and Literary Institution Papers, 1826–1871*, Manuscript, State Library of New South Wales, A1625.
75. *Catalogue*, MPL, 1861, viii: http://www.ucd.ie/southhem/record.html#112.
76. Quoted in Richard Overell, 'The Melbourne Public Library and the Guillaumes: The Relations between a Colonial Library and its London Book Supplier, 1854–1865', in *Peopling a Profession: Papers from the Fourth Forum on Australian Library History*, ed. Frank Upward and Jean P. Whyte (Melbourne: Ancora Press, 1991), 33–63 (43).
77. For the figure of 650 seats, see McVilly, '"Something to Blow About"?', 82. P. R. Harris, 'The British Museum Library 1857–1973', in *The Cambridge History of Libraries in Great Britain and Ireland Volume III 1850–2000*, ed. Alistair Black and Peter Hoare (Cambridge: Cambridge University Press, 2006), 281–298 (282).
78. Barry, *Address on the Opening of The Free Public Library of Ballarat East*, 16–18.
79. Geoffrey Sherington, *Australia's Immigrants 1788–1978* (Sydney: George Allen & Unwin, 1980), 59; James Belich, *Replenishing the Earth: The Settler Revolution and the Rise of the Angloworld* (Oxford: Oxford University Press, 2009), 309–312.
80. For a similar view of New Zealand's progress, see J. E. Traue, 'A Paradise for Readers? The Extraordinary Proliferation of Public Libraries in Colonial New Zealand', *Script & Print: Bulletin of the Bibliographical Society of Australia and New Zealand* 29 (2005): 323–340 (332).
81. *Straits Times*, September 30, 1846, 3.
82. David Goodman, *Gold Seeking: Victoria and California in the 1850s* (Stanford: Stanford University Press, 1994), 87.
83. *Herald* (Melbourne), March 28, 1862, 4.
84. *South Australian Weekly Chronicle* (Adelaide), September 2, 1866, 4.
85. *Argus*, July 14, 1855, 4.
86. *Argus*, October 27, 1856, 2.
87. *The South Australian Institute… Addresses Delivered at the Laying of the Foundation Stone*, 17.
88. Joyce, 'Politics of the Liberal Archive', 44.
89. *South Australian Register*, October 18, 1859, 5.
90. See, for example, *South Australian Register*, September 7, 1859, 3.
91. Joyce, 'Politics of the Liberal Archive', 42.
92. On the loggia design, see *Argus*, July 6, 1855, 5, and Brian Hubber, 'Leading by Example: Barry in the Library', *La Trobe Journal* 73 (2004): 67–74 (68–69).

93. *Argus*, September 10, 1866, 6. See also Redmond Barry, *Address to the Workmen Employed in Building the Great Hall of the Melbourne Public Library and Museum in Melbourne, Victorian* (Melbourne: Wilson & Mackinnon, 1866).
94. Bain Attwood and Helen Doyle, *Possession: Batman's Treaty and the Matter of History* (Carlton, Vic: Miegunyah Press, 2009), 134.
95. *Catalogue*, SAPL, 1829: http://www.ucd.ie/southhem/record.html#264.
96. *Catalogue*, SAPL, 1842: http://www.ucd.ie/southhem/record.html#269.
97. *Catalogue*, SAPL, 1862: http://www.ucd.ie/southhem/record.html#270.
98. *Straits Times*, September 30, 1846, 3.
99. *General Catalogue of Bound Volumes in the Raffles Library*, September 1, 1877 (Singapore: s.n., 1877), n.p.
100. Gaunt, 'Identity and Nation in the Australian Public Library', 33, 43–51.
101. *South Australian Weekly Chronicle*, October 19, 1861, 3.
102. *Catalogue*, SALMI, 1848: http://www.ucd.ie/southhem/record.html#49; *Catalogue*, SAI, 1869: http://www.ucd.ie/southhem/record.html#188.
103. Heather Gaunt, '"To do things for the good of others": Library Philanthropy, William Walker, and the Establishment of the Australiana Collection at the Tasmanian Public Library in the 1920s and 1930s', *The Australian Library Journal* 56, no. 3/4 (2007): 251–264.
104. Gaunt, 'Identity and Nation in the Australian Public Library', 43–45.
105. See G. D. Richardson, 'Mitchell, David Scott (1836–1907)', *ADNB*, accessed 14 November 2018: http://adb.anu.edu.au/biography/mitchell-david-scott-4210.
106. Graeme Johanson, *A Study of Colonial Editions in Australia, 1843–1972* (Wellington: Elibank Press, 2000).
107. Quoted in Gaunt, 'Identity and Nation in the Australian Public Library', 44.
108. *Herald*, September 20, 1874, 2; *Austral Review*, Aug 1877, 2; *Age*, January 27, 1879, 2. See McVilly, '"Something to Blow About"?', 87.
109. John Dunham, 'The British India Holdings of the State Library of Victoria', *La Trobe Journal* 16 (1975): 77–88 (78, 81).
110. Dunham, 'British India Holdings', 84.
111. *Herald*, August 21, 1861, 5.
112. *Argus*, June 26, 1867, 7.
113. Dunham, 'British India Holdings', 77.

Open Access This chapter is licensed under the terms of the Creative Commons Attribution 4.0 International License (http://creativecommons.org/licenses/by/4.0/), which permits use, sharing, adaptation, distribution and reproduction in any medium or format, as long as you give appropriate credit to the original author(s) and the source, provide a link to the Creative Commons licence and indicate if changes were made.

The images or other third party material in this chapter are included in the chapter's Creative Commons licence, unless indicated otherwise in a credit line to the material. If material is not included in the chapter's Creative Commons licence and your intended use is not permitted by statutory regulation or exceeds the permitted use, you will need to obtain permission directly from the copyright holder.

CHAPTER 3

Cultivating Public Readers: Citizens, Classes, and Types

Abstract This chapter considers readers in the southern colonies, from various constructions of reader types to the class, gender, and racial composition of colonial reading publics. Locating the users of colonial public libraries within discourses that include sexuality, morality, citizenship, race, and class, the chapter looks at the ways in which public libraries contributed both to expanded understandings of the term 'public' and to the management of colonial class and race relations, thereby reflecting and redefining the boundaries of citizenship in emerging colonial polities.

Keywords Reading publics • Working-class readers • Loafers • Women readers • Indigenous readers

Patrick Joyce has argued that the rise of free municipal libraries in Britain in the mid- to late-nineteenth century was essential to the emergence of a 'new vocabulary of the social', particularly as it related to revised and expanded understandings of the term 'public'. The idea of a free institution funded by the public purse meant that the individual subject was not so much attached to different voluntary organisations or to the market or even to the state, but rather to a new sense of ordinary communal citizenship grounded in liberal and, increasingly, democratic values. In contrast to the earlier efforts of subscription libraries to consolidate middle-class and elite values, the British public library movement was to give the working classes free access to the public realm, thereby 'constituting it as demotic'.[1] A similar trajectory towards new forms of liberal, democratic citizenship can be traced via the library history of the southern colonies, but the self-improvement culture of the British public library movement nonetheless had to be adapted and modified in the colonial context. Accounting for, among other things, the education of Indigenous, mixed-race, and multi-ethnic populations, different forms and conditions of white and Indigenous labour, and the accelerated developmental pace of colonial societies would require locally specific understandings and conceptions of the term 'public' as the nineteenth century progressed. It would also require public libraries to address and account for particular kinds and classes of readers from diggers, bushmen, and Indigenous populations to squatters, tradesmen, and urban elites.

If, as Michael Warner has argued, a public exists only by virtue of being 'addressed in discourse' or, in other words, as 'a space of (discursive) circulation', the ways in which public libraries cultivated and/or excluded certain types of readers were essential to developing colonial identity formations.[2] David Wittenberg has rightly noted that '[t]o be part of a public, to be part of *the* public, is to be at once both an actor and a stand-in'.[3] Public libraries were not, therefore, only social spaces where actual readers could physically congregate, but also discursive spaces in which local presses and library management committees could cultivate ideal reading types that reflected the social values to which emerging colonial polities aspired. In so far as available source material permits, this chapter addresses colonial reading publics in both a notional and an empirical sense, looking at the ways in which reading communities in the colonies reflected the practices of actual readers and the construction of reader archetypes. Reader types, like character types, can be defined as what Ken Gelder, Rachael Weaver, and Elizabeth Fowler have called 'models of social identity' or 'social persons' that act as analogues of real persons.[4] Depictions of colonial readers of every class and type, from diletantish 'loungers', unemployed 'loafers', and 'careless skimmers of the last romance' to scholars, blue-stockings, and 'curious annotators in the library of reference', therefore represent a kind of constructed sociology of colonial life, one that—perhaps even more than actual readerships—was used to define and police the boundaries of citizenship in the southern colonies.[5]

Working and Middle-Class Readers

In a revealing letter to the *Sydney Morning Herald* in 1869, an anonymous 'Reader' argued that a truly public library would be freely circulating so as to cater for the needs of the 'mass of the population', who 'have to read by snatches of time; many at hours when a public library *could* not be open'.[6] Concluding that the establishment of a reference library in Sydney would result in the persistence of the kind of closed '*coterie[s]* of professed *littérateurs*' that haunted both the BML and the MPL,[7] the correspondent noted that '[t]he people who can go into a public library in the day time are not *the public*' but rather the leisure classes and other elites. The correspondent's association of the 'public' with the working 'masses' rather than with the gentlemanly leisure classes points, most obviously, to new understandings of the public as the ordinary working people, but it is also suggestive of the relationship between expanded definitions of the term and democratic suffrage. A 'mere public library without a loan arrangement', argued the correspondent, would be of 'little use *to the masses*, in whose hands we have placed the franchise, and in whose hands we should place first-class books'.[8]

While it is hard to be sure of the class and gender locations of anonymous correspondents to newspapers, who often used pseudonyms and engaged in complex acts of subject positioning, the primarily middle-class readership of newspapers such as the *Sydney Morning Herald* is suggestive of the extent to which the colonial middle classes saw their own societies as (potentially) more egalitarian than those of the metropoles. This sense of democratic potential even permeated the book acquisition policies of library management committees. In 1879, the SAI particularly regretted that its reference collection was deficient in works of 'constitutional history, polity and their allied subjects' because South Australia was 'a democratic community and enjoying universal suffrage'.[9] In arguing for increased book provision for the working classes, the anonymous correspondent also assumes the high literacy competencies of colonial working-class populations: all they require, he argues, is free access to 'first-class books'. Studies of literacy in emigration populations in mid-nineteenth-century Australia do indeed point to higher educational attainments among emigrants from Britain and Ireland in comparison to their respective regional home populations. This is true both of convicts and free settlers, and was particularly pronounced in the colonies of New South Wales and Victoria.[10] In 1862, Victoria's literacy rate was 'twice that of Britain's, far higher than London's or any other colony's, and one of the highest in the world'.[11] Kathleen Fennessy estimates that by 1881 95% of people of both sexes in Victoria could read and 88% could write.[12] According to the 1865 census in the Cape Colony, 65.7% of whites in the Western Cape were literate and 63.9% in the Eastern Cape, whereas only 9.7% of the black and African populations could read.[13] In Singapore, nineteenth-century literacy rates among the small, largely middle-class white populations were high but, even by 1921, literacy rates among the whole population (primarily Malays and Chinese) were only 36.6% for all languages and 8.3% for English.[14]

Despite the relatively high literacy rates among European settlers, it is difficult to know from the available sources how many working-class readers frequented public libraries in the southern colonies or what they read. Ann L. Stoler has rightly argued that the 'presence of poor whites in the colonies was far more widespread than most colonial histories lead us to imagine',[15] but the white working-class population was negligible in the southern hemisphere in all but the Australian and New Zealand colonies. Franchise colonies such as the Cape Colony, where Indigenous and local populations far outweighed settler populations, tended to use local, immigrant, or indentured labour rather than white working-class labour. In the Cape, a shortage of skilled working-class labourers was a constant complaint, and debates about the introduction of a lower third rate of subscription at the SAPL in 1848 were framed around the need to make the library accessible to lower-middle-class professionals rather than the working classes.[16] The SAPL was therefore nearly exclusively the domain of middle-class white men, including a relatively large number of 'gentlemen from India' (generally civil servants on leave from Bengal) and 'military in garrison' who were considered prestigious additions to the library's membership, and swelled otherwise fairly small and static subscription numbers.[17] The small artisanal working-class population in Cape Town was primarily served by Alexander Jardine's Popular Library.[18] In Singapore, the white working class was even smaller than in the Cape, and the SL and RLM were also predominantly used by the white middle classes. The introduction of a cheaper library subscription rate in 1847 saw an increase in the number of female subscribers and lower-middle-class administrators but did not substantially change the demographic of the SL's users.[19]

The Australian colonies, on the other hand, had relatively high numbers of both skilled and unskilled labourers, many of whom were encouraged by the gold-rush emigration of the 1850s.[20] In colonial Tasmania, for example, the 1870 census, published the year the TPL opened, provides a four-tiered structure of professional/commercial class (5%), middle-class waged (20%), industrial class (34%), and labouring class (41%).[21] The subscription and circulation figures of public libraries in colonial Australia unfortunately provide little indication of the class or gender proportions of library users, and references to working-class readers are largely anecdotal. The Melbourne *Herald* claimed that the MPL's Queen's Reading Room was 'crowded with persons of all classes', but provides no sense of the number of readers from each class.[22] The *Age* stated that most of the MPL's readers were 'bona fide workers', while the *Australasian* claimed that the library was 'largely used by the better class of artisans' and that 'many men studied the science of their occupation'. It appears from press comments such as these that the bulk of the MPL's users were the 'lower middle classes, clerks, professional men and skilled artisans' rather than the working classes or the upper middle classes, the latter of whom were wealthy enough to have their own private libraries.[23]

The Sydney FPL's early users, on the other hand, appear to have been primarily working class, with the library's trustees noting in their report for 1877 that 'an erroneous impression had formerly prevailed that the institution was simply a reading-room and a library for the working classes' rather than 'a Public State Library for all classes'. If by 1878 the FPL was being 'extensively used by students of all classes', including those 'persons of superior culture, who formerly kept away', the library does seem to have been used by readers who would normally have been members of mechanics' institutes.[24] In 1856, the SAI noted that 'we are … assured—in fact, numerous autographs in the "Application Book" prove the statement—that our rural settlers and bushmen are taking great interest in the establishment', suggesting that the non-urban working class was at least visiting the library during trips to the city. At the other extreme, an article on mechanics' institutes in the *Mount Alexander Mail* (Castlemaine, Victoria) claimed that 'a prejudice exists in the Melbourne Public Library, against anything hailing from the diggings, and the feeling was some time ago offensively manifested by the ejection from the reading room of two miners who had the audacity to appear in their woollen jumpers in that repository of wisdom'.[25]

Notwithstanding the commitment of public libraries to universal adult education, the alleged ejection of inappropriately dressed diggers from the MPL is suggestive of the extent to which such libraries were markers of middle-class respectability. Establishing hierarchies of readers from the 'imperious Fitzjones, of the Civil service' to 'Smith, his carpenter', the conservative Melbourne *Herald* suggested in 1875, for example, that while the 'perfect freedom of entrance' associated with the MPL was in theory pleasing to a 'democratic community', it had its limits. 'Much could be forgiven', the *Herald* argued, 'if the Library were rendered a little more pleasant for the decent and cleanly classes'.[26] Decent working-class men and women or the 'honest labouring poor' were therefore differentiated from the under-class of loafers, vagabonds, and other types of 'undeserving' poor discussed later in this chapter, but they were not immune from scrutiny, particularly in relation to complaints about the overcrowding of the library. In a parody of negative representations of working-class readers in conservative papers, *Melbourne Punch* depicts a bunch of 'tailors of a studious turn' who are seated on the floor like 'Turks' and to whom 'the paucity of chairs is of little importance', resulting in the paper's ongoing tongue-in-cheek concern with the vulgarity of public facilities: '"Public" stands, in short, for vulgar—for instance take a few / Public cases—"public houses", "public men" and—"women", too!'.[27]

Punch plays here on fears that public libraries and other public spaces might become places of ill-repute, encouraging the kind of vulgar behaviour associated with inebriated men and loose women. Public libraries certainly drew on the rhetoric of respectability, family life, and domestic economy in order to regulate the use of their spaces, encouraging personal habits such as good hygiene and ventilation, habits of temperance, economy and time management, and disciplined reading practices in their users in an attempt to incorporate such users into the 'larger social structures' of family, work, and community. Conferring both social stigma and an opportunity to overcome it, public libraries were therefore alert to the 'pedagogic functions of reading' and their potential effect on a broad range of social behaviours.[28]

Mary Hammond has noted, in the British context, the extent to which the reader was constructed through class-inflected routines as well as 'through the social functions linked to the public spaces in which books were selected, displayed, and read'.[29] While the *Herald* imagined Fitzjones (the civil servant) and Smith (his carpenter) reading side-by-side, the very ceremony of signing one's name or requesting books from librarians could be off-putting to working-class and lower-middle-class readers, as could the size and scale of public buildings, the new competencies required to navigate modern catalogues and access policies, and the rarefied practices of silent and solitary reading. There is evidence to suggest that Redmond Barry intended the portico entrance of the MPL's classical building, added in 1870, to be a mediatory architectural device linking street and interior, people and books,[30] but in an article in 1867, *Melbourne Punch* portrays the 'great Antipodean Lyceum' as a 'sacred fence' or gateway to knowledge that is eminently unwelcoming to the unsuspecting 'stranger'. First being forced to meet 'the lazy and passive stare of the policeman at the door' who is there to prevent the theft of books, the would-be reader is then required to write his name in a book. Rejecting that as 'an unwarranted intrusion of the liberty of the subject', *Punch*'s reader walks along the 'silent cocoanut matting' to the washbasin to wash his hands surrounded by 'casts of certain ancient chef d'oivres' and 'prints of Raphael's cartoons'. The increasingly dirty towel mounted on a roller by the double-barrelled hand-wash apparatus provides, *Punch* jokes, a 'goodly lesson' and 'is doubtless provided by the trustees for the purposes of showing what may be effected by indomitable energy and praiseworthy perseverance'. Finally, at the door to the reading room, the visitor is given 'a neat little lecture on social ethics—he is told—to take off his hat!'.[31]

These kinds of rules and rituals surrounding the use of library spaces are not only suggestive of middle-class pressures on the working classes to dress and act a certain way, but also served to turn the library-going public into a kind of 'public police'. As Redmond Barry acknowledged in his address at the opening of the Ballarat Free Public Library in 1869, the point of library regulations relating to dress, cleanliness, and behaviour was to encourage 'social conformity', although he was emphatically against the seemingly 'insatiable desire' for 'superintending the studies' of readers.[32] The 'social psychology' of the nineteenth-century library as a disciplinary space was also evident in the ways in which library spaces were organised, from the display of busts of prominent liberal thinkers and ornamental books to the open, radial 'palatial design' of reading rooms, which enabled both 'the chance to view the giant structure of knowledge as a whole' and the panoramic viewing of the many by the many.[33] A more explicit form of surveillance came both from the policemen stationed at the front of libraries such as the MPL and the SAI to prevent the theft of books, and from library staff. 'A Visitor to the Public Library' in 1863 proposed for the MPL a system already in place in 'the large free libraries of Liverpool and Manchester', namely, a slip recording a borrower's address and the number of the book borrowed. Such a system, the correspondent argued, would ensure that 'a check is placed on each reader that enters the room'.[34] A similar method of recording borrowings in a designated book was introduced at the SL from the outset, along with an inspection of returned books by the librarian.[35]

These kinds of 'bureauropathetic behavior[s]' or 'checks', along with other forms of surveillance, were a large part of a librarian's role in the nineteenth century.[36] As the *South Australian Weekly Chronicle* noted in a debate on the merits of free access to library shelves, the books at the SAI 'are directly under the charge of the Librarian, Mr. P. S. Benham, and no person is allowed access to them on the shelves except for purposes of reference or study'.[37] Such service-oriented procedures allowed librarians to supervise, track, and monitor users, as well as to record their activities in registers and logbooks. Even readers at the open access MPL remained under the 'direct physical observation' of library staff.[38] In a parody of the overinflated self-importance of the MPL reader in 1864, *Melbourne Punch* noted that 'Mr A. Wake's' daily visits were often disturbed by the sub-librarian, who, 'regardless of the profundity of his cogitations, says—"You must not sleep here!"'.[39]

The censoring of books was an additional form of middle-class surveillance and control. Comparing the governing committee of the SAI to a 'conclave' of 'high-priests of literature', the *South Australian Weekly Chronicle* argued that no group of people should 'decide dogmatically what the colony may read and what the colony may not', and that censorship in a 'national library' was 'opposed to the tendencies of modern thought'.[40] The *Chronicle*'s view that a national library should include even dangerous reading material was echoed in Singapore, where Brendan Luyt has shown that the RLM contained fiction which had been censored in many American and British libraries.[41] Most public libraries in the colonies were, however, concerned with the moral character of their collections, and attempted to provide their readers with improving material and only the best kind of 'standard' fiction (see Chap. 4). In many ways, this was the result of their middle-class governance structures. While the liberal principles of public libraries supported free access as far as respectability and social decorum would allow, their governance was almost invariably in the hands of coteries of propertied men of public, professional, or commercial distinction, giving these men a very significant role as colonial censors and knowledge brokers. The boards of trustees of public libraries therefore operated almost as an extension of the predilection for a genteel club life dominated by ethnic, ideological, or religious kinship, which was one of Britain's most distinctive cultural exports to its colonies.[42] Before the professionalisation of library studies, chief librarians, too, tended to be middle-class males like Augustus Tulk and Alexander Jardine, suggesting the gendered and class-inflected recruitment patterns of equally male-dominated library governance committees.

The potentially levelling function of the public library as an open, meritocratic institution must therefore be set against the fact that such libraries were generally run by, and catered for, a select middle-class public, who engaged in various forms of paternalism, censorship, and surveillance, and whose interests were often removed from working-class auto-didactic cultures and from the needs of the general public in its new expanded sense.[43] As in Britain, the colonial public library became, more often than not, what Hammond has called an 'architecturally repressive and logistically prohibitive symbol of civic pride patronized overwhelmingly by the lower middle classes'. It was a space, in other words, 'that ended up militating against large sections of the population whom it had been intended to serve'.[44]

Loungers, Loafers, and Idlers

Some of the greatest nuisances faced by the colonial public library, according to the local press, were the characters of the lounger and loafer. Depictions of loungers and loafers ranged from providing a source of entertainment and mockery, to being seen as a public irritant, and finally, to being viewed as a danger to public order and respectability. *Melbourne Punch*, for example, got significant mileage out of the loafer character as a means of mocking the content of the MPL's collections as well as its lofty designs as a national institution for public education. In a squib titled 'Sleeping Arrangements', *Punch* announced that the MPL was now accepting 'loafers and others' in its 'commodious and well ventilated building' for a 'comfortable doze any time from ten a.m. to ten p.m.', adding that '[b]ooks calculated to induce somnolency can be had on application'.[45] Most letters and editorials concerning the lounging and loafing class were not, however, as amused by their presence in the library, with the Melbourne *Argus* writing that '[y]ou will inevitably be distracted if you have sitting close by you an unpleasant-looking street lounger, perhaps with suspicious restlessness turning over books you want to consult, perhaps breathing heavily in sleep, but in either case redolent of uncleanliness and gin'.[46] Increasingly, the library became a battleground for middle-class sensibilities and, although lounger and loafer were initially terms used interchangeably, the lounger became a more benign 'idler' while the loafer came to assume a more insidious figure associated with the unemployed and criminal lower classes.[47]

Coupled with 'light reading' (see Chap. 4), if any reading at all, the presence of loungers and loafers in the public library was a much-debated topic, even if, in reality, the number of loafers was probably small and confined to a few repeat offenders. In a letter to the Philosophical Society of Queensland, Redmond Barry noted that book purchases for the MPL were specifically designed to dissuade these characters by 'admitting no works of a trivial or ephemeral character, which, serve merely to dissipate the idle hours of the lounger'.[48] In 1856, the Melbourne *Age* similarly pointed to the scholarly, and somewhat dour, nature of the MPL's original collection as a safeguard against both loungers and improper, frivolous reading practices, insisting that 'on no account … must the Library be made a mere lounging room for casual readers of magazines and newspapers, or a circulating library for the lovers of cheap fictions'. While nominally supporting the principles of free public access, it supposed that maintaining an ambitious, universalist focus would in itself ensure that patronage would be appropriately limited to the 'few' colonial cognoscenti or 'zealous devotees of literature who haunt its quiet and grateful precincts'.[49] By 1860, the *Age* noted that its prescription had not come to pass, and complained that the institution had instead become 'the paradise of loafers and loungers, who completely subvert the actual uses and intents of the place'.[50]

Although the male loafer—women were accused of many crimes in the library, but loafing was not one of them—found his way into libraries in other southern colonies, as well as in North America and Britain, the MPL was viewed as particularly vulnerable to loafers because its shelves were open access, it had generous opening hours, and it was open to anyone over the age of 14. As David McVilly notes in his history of the MPL, during the 1860s and 1870s 'hardly a month passed without an editorial writer or letter-writer complaining of loafers and loungers who used the Library for amusement purposes rather than for the serious purposes for which it was intended'.[51] McVilly rightly argues that the representation in the local newspapers of these undesired library users most often came from the pen of the middle classes, and that 'admirers of the Library seem to have overreacted to its possible misuse' and fully subscribed to the 'utilitarian and puritanical principles on which it was based'.[52]

To the most militant of observers, these characters threatened to undermine not only the utility, respectability, and perceived purpose of the public library, but also the very productivity of the colony itself. The *Argus* wondered if the MPL was too much of a 'temptation', and if access to the library was made more select then the 'array of loafers' might find 'some occupation more beneficial to society and to themselves'. In contrast to the argument in favour of public libraries as providing opportunities for self-improvement and rational recreation for the working classes, the *Argus* proposed a cost-benefit analysis of the public good offered by the MPL, asking whether the '"little knowledge", proverbially dangerous, which they acquire … can in any way compensate a community such as ours for the loss of so many vigorous arms, and what might otherwise be so many honest toil-stained hands?'[53] During his address at the opening of a mechanics' institute in New South Wales, the pastoralist Gideon Lang also raised the question of utility, identifying three classes of workers with the third class being 'the loafers, a set of lazy ruffians, of every grade, count, and occupation, who came out originally to the diggings because unfit for any steady, industrious pursuit at home, and for the same reason had taken advantage of the system of "loafing" prevailing in the pastoral districts to become vagabonds'.[54]

The loafer figure could appear in numerous guises—from Lang's pastoral figure to the metropolitan 'ruffian'—but, as Michael Zakim has argued in the North American context, its 'omnipresence' in the public mind 'was testimony to an emerging labor problem: a crisis in the meaning of industriousness that had been provoked, aptly enough, by an industrial revolution'.[55] As in North America, the 'problem of the loafer' was increasingly viewed in the southern colonies as a class issue driven by unemployed, indolent labour. Although unemployment would not become acute in the Australian colonies until the severe depression of the 1890s, the boom–bust cycles of the gold rush had, according to Marx, led to the early 'glut of the Australian labour market' and the peripatetic men the gold diggings attracted were viewed with increasing anxiety.[56] Criticisms levelled by the *Age* against the MPL for allowing access to these loafers was not solely because the library was wasted on them, but also because they discouraged more respectable readers from using the library by occupying tables and chairs. The unwanted and unwashed loafer is often contrasted with the 'studious', industrious, and respectable student who is in the library to pursue 'systematic study' or to make 'references and extracts for literary uses'.[57] The loafer was thus seen to pose a threat to serious intellectual endeavours and the progress of the colony. The *Argus* urged that a separate room with 'greater facilities for note-making' be created for the 'better kind of students, supplied with writing materials, served by one or two attendants, and open only to those who can give evidence of a serious intention'.[58]

Loafers were accused of further impeding serious study by damaging and stealing the library's books. Frequent appeals were made to the benefits of the reading card application system of the BML, which, if adopted in Melbourne, would be a 'means of excluding a class whose room is better than their company, while it would offer no real impediment to the well-intentioned reader'.[59] Although most newspaper reports associated the damage and theft of books with loafers or the working classes, some like an article in the *Herald* came to their defence, arguing instead that the loafer's 'malodorousness, his unclean fingers, his general qualities of unwashedness are only lightly objectionable, compared with the determined vandalism of the respectable and educated frequenter of that most admirable institution'.[60] *Melbourne Punch* lampooned the tendency to blame the 'carbonaceous deposit' accumulated on the skin of the 'sons of toil' for the soiling of books by drawing 'a connection between mechanical knowledge and mechanical dirt'. Punning on the self-help culture of the public library movement, *Punch* jokes that 'it is these self-helping gentlemen who soil the books'.[61]

Complaints about the damage of books by unwashed hands of all classes were certainly frequent, with a report in the *South Australian Weekly Chronicle* criticising the state of books at the SALMI, where 'should a person desire to look up a passage in the works of any leading author ... it will probably be in a filthy state of grease and dirt, reeking of tobacco smoke or stale beer, and possibly containing marginal notes made by aspiring youths with greasy fingers'.[62] The damage done to books by smoking was also remarked upon in the 1850 SAPL report and in the *Cape of Good Hope Literary Gazette*, which pointed to 'that numerous race of careless unthinking' despoilers, from 'bed-readers' and 'segar smokers' to 'coffee drinkers' and 'general loungers', noting that 'not the least of the aggressors' are 'those who scribble with the pen or pencil, and record the marginal nonsense of their *own composing*'.[63] The frequent lamentations about the abuse of books by colonial newspapers and libraries alike can occasionally give us glimpses into what was being read, with the *Herald* reporting that the 'volumes of the dramatists are dirtied and mutilated to a disgraceful extent', and that the 'favourite authors of the "loafing" fraternity' were 'the more licentious specimens of the literature of the Elizabethan and succeeding periods'. Volumes of Walter Scott and Dryden are both recorded as being 'mutilated', while 'Massinger Ford, and a few others, are thumbed and torn, and so of course, is "Don Juan"'.[64]

The middle-class obsession with overcrowding and cleanliness, and in particular with the requirement that readers wash their hands before entering the MPL, was the target of a number of *Melbourne Punch* articles, some of which pointed out that hand-washing encouraged the very loafers that the library was seeking to discourage. A *Punch* illustration from 1887, for example, shows the MPL's chief librarian from 1881 to 1895, Thomas Francis Bride, angling for 'soap stealers' and catching three 'very queer fish', all of whom are clearly undesirable loafers (Fig. 3.1).[65] While the

Fig. 3.1 'While There's Life There's Soap', wood engraving, *Melbourne Punch*, January 13, 1887, 15. Courtesy of Trove: https://trove.nla.gov.au/newspaper/page/20442557

constant references in the press to unwashed loafers and the repeated complaints about soap being stolen from the library reveal the class tensions unfolding within the walls of the public library, uncleanliness did pose a significant problem—and not only to the books. Calling the loafer a 'practical entomologist', the *Herald* points to the fear of insect- and pest-carrying individuals but also to the concern that books could spread diseases.[66] Alexander Black has noted in the British context the extent to which the massification of the library and its wider role as a 'clinic' for social diseases led to exaggerated fears about the spread of physical diseases via both germs from dirty hands and atmospheric impurities or poor ventilation in shared spaces.[67]

Pathologising dirtiness was, of course, a form of social control designed to keep out those deemed undesirable. As Harald Fischer-Tiné has argued, loafers posed a 'latent threat to [European] civilising ambitions' and could lower 'European prestige' by blurring the hierarchies between coloniser and colonised. Efforts to police the 'transgressive' loafers in the MPL therefore became part of an 'internal civilising mission'. Encouraging clean hands was ostensibly meant to preserve books, but it was also a way of discouraging vagabonds and those in manual labour or the 'dirty professions', as well as consolidating the public library space as one primarily for the 'decent', cleanly lower middle classes who 'conform[ed] to civilised habits'.[68]

Women Readers

A parody letter written to the *Sydney Morning Herald* in 1844 indicates the figurative power of the woman novel reader who frequents the library. Signed 'Lavinia Readmuch', the writer identifies herself as a 'subscriber to the Australian Subscription Library' and describes her discriminate reading habits as 'being rather choice ... I do not on an average read above six novels a week, with the occasional dip into a new poem—when there is such a thing'. The complaint 'Readmuch' levels against the ASL is that smokers are ruining her reading experience: 'some of the nasty creatures read novels when they are smoking—and the consequence is, that ... the whole book becomes impregnated with tobacco, until it smells as bad as a tobacconist's shop'. Whether the letter-writer is using the figure of the woman reader to criticise the practice of smoking—as noted above, a common concern of library management committees—or simply mocking the criticism itself, it nonetheless demonstrates the potency of the woman reader encroaching on male space. Her reading habits are frivolous: the reading of six novels a week does not indicate a serious or considered reading practice and sexual innuendos litter the text. On appealing to the ASL committee to end the nasty habit of smoking, 'Readmuch' writes: 'do your best to put an end to it, there's good souls; and if you succeed, I'll (but I musn't say what I'll do, for it will look like bribery)'.[69]

The licentious, ravenous novel reader was not the only type of female reader satirised for attending the colonial public library. As early as 1841, the SAPL recognised another female presence: that of the colonial bluestocking. Stressing the need for the SAPL to appeal both to the serious student and the general reader, 'uniting the instruction with the recreation of the mind', Advocate Musgrove argued that 'we are not all equally gifted, or destined to explore the paths of literature and science. It is not everyone who reads merely for the sake of being edified, nor is it every lady who wishes to become a Blue Stocking'.[70] An 1868 *Melbourne Punch* article describing the 'women of the time' in Melbourne draws a mocking portrait of the colonial blue-stocking: 'an awfully well-read young lady' who had 'been a governess; but owing to paternal speculations in gold mines having curiously enough turned out successfully, she has relinquished the drudgery of teaching'. The blue-stocking is much too serious for novel reading, with the *Punch* writer 'feeling abashed' that he 'was carrying home Miss BRADDON's last novel' while she was reading 'Ecce Homo and Darwin's Species'. Spending 'most of her time in the Public Library', the blue-stocking occupies a different, but equally troubling, position in the male-dominated space of the library as the female novel reader. As we can see from the parody in Fig. 3.2, women occupy all the seats in the science section—'she knows ever so much of botany, conchology, paleontology'—and they thus both distract and prevent the learned gentleman from taking his seat and pursuing the scientific studies necessary for the benefit of the colony as a whole.[71]

Given the club-like, rule-bound, 'manifestly exclusive' sociability of the subscription library model, it is unsurprising that women faced restricted access to many colonial institutions in the first half of the nineteenth century.[72] No women were among the 74 founding subscriber-proprietors of the ASL in 1826, though the library had not seen it necessary to add to the many rules of the institution by prohibiting them. By the time it was decided that 'ladies' could be admitted to the ranks of subscribers by the normal balloting process in 1846, a number of women had already become proprietors by virtue of widowhood or other inheritances.[73] There was just one woman among the 124 founding subscribers of the TPL in 1849, and none

Fig. 3.2 'At the Public Library', wood engraving, *Australasian Sketcher*, February 23, 1888, Courtesy of the State Library of Victoria: http://handle.slv.vic.gov.au/10381/258786

among the founders of the SL a few years earlier.[74] By the 1870s, however, a Miss Little is recorded in the list of proprietors of the SL, the first reference to a female proprietor.[75] Women were not admitted to the SAPL in its original incarnation, but did come to assert their presence during its phase as a public subscription library. The Attorney General William Porter compared the behaviour of 'some ladies' in the SAPL with Miss Lucy Slattern from Sheridan's *The Rivals* (1775), who 'has the most observing thumb' and 'cherishes her nails for the convenience of making marginal notes'.[76] In 1853, the then Governor of the Cape Colony, Harry Smith, was mildly disturbed that women as well as men were attending the subscribers' meetings, noting that 'while we cordially admit that their "presence civilizes ours" it has nevertheless long been, and will long, I trust, continue to be, the custom of our country, both for their sakes as well as our own, to exclude from what we may term the "public business" of life'.[77]

Despite these difficult beginnings, female participation in public reading culture and literary sociability in the southern colonies was gradually normalised, and eventually, if paternalistically, encouraged. The ALSMI actively sought the attendance of women at their social literary events, and during an 1840 meeting a special appeal was made to women to continue supporting the institute through their presence:

> I implore them, as the brightest ornaments of this their adopted land, to aid us further by persuasion—still by example. In such a cause and with such advocates, the barren waste of human ignorance would quickly be transformed to the cultivated garden of knowledge—the forest would resound to the axe—the hunter would advance—the desert would indeed bloom and blossom as the rose.[78]

As with many mechanics' institutes in the Australian colonies, the ALSMI recognised that women could be used as 'marker[s] of respectability' not only for their social events but for the institute's reputation as a whole.[79] The expectation that women would attend the social events of the institution continued under the SAI as the rules noted that a subscriber's annual 30-shilling fee 'empowers him to introduce two ladies, or two children, to the lectures or *conversaziones* of the society'.[80]

The TPL records provide attendance figures for both men and women, and while the number of women users of the library were significantly less than men, the library's six-month reports show a steady increase of women frequenting the library, from 540 in 1860 to 630 in 1861, 637 in 1862, and 659 in 1863.[81] The MPL marked its liberal principles with the addition of a 'Ladies area' in the new wing of the building opened in 1859.[82] Female readers, moreover, were not denied any of the access rights enjoyed by men, and by 1874, the *Herald* praised the 'courageous ladies' who had colonised the library:

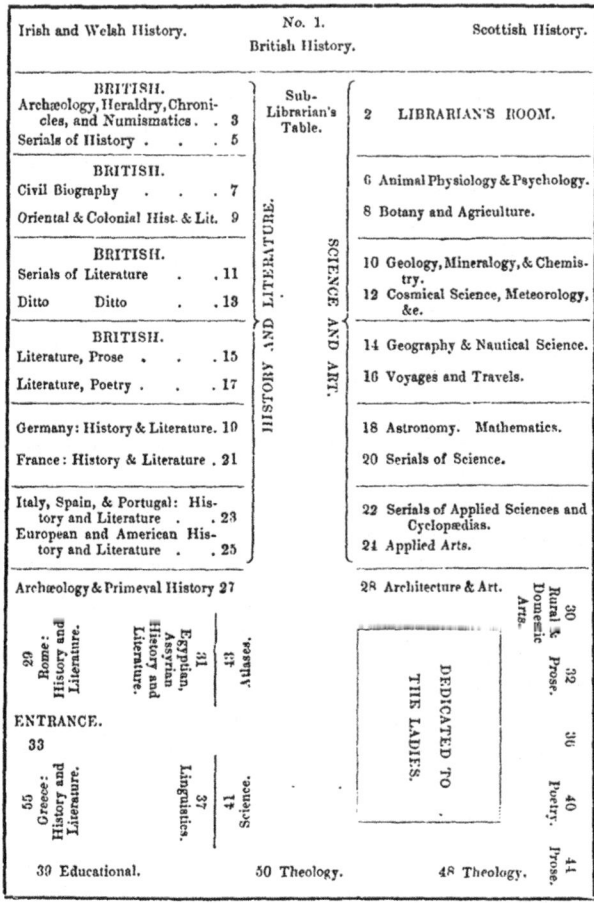

Fig. 3.3 'Synopsis of the Public Library', *Catalogue*, MPL, 1861, xvi. Courtesy of BCCSH and the State Library of Victoria: http://www.ucd.ie/southhem/record.html#112

helping themselves to books from various quarters in the library, and sitting down to read where they find it most convenient; expressing a tacit dissent from the idea that they should confine themselves to a 'ladies room', furnished with picture books, suitable to their limited understandings.

The *Herald* even suggested that 'ladies asserting their right to use the library with the same freedom as others' would be the best antidote to loungers and loafers as '[t]hey will feel it so extremely awkward indulging in their grunts and snoozes'.[83] In Singapore, both the SL and RLM were similarly seen as a necessary public amenity for attracting white women to the tropics, who could safeguard against the degeneration of young men. The RLM was therefore 'conceived as a public space suitable for women'.[84]

The public library was also viewed as providing 'positive protection' for working-class women, who, because of their colonial setting, were 'without any family connections'. During the debate over Sunday opening hours at the MPL, a letter to the *Argus* argued in favour of Sunday opening for the 'many hundreds of servants, milliners' assistants, shop women, and other females who have no time at all to read any books during week days'.[85] Similar claims were made in relation to an attempt to decrease the evening opening hours of the FPL in Sydney.[86] Another letter to the editor claimed that opening on a Sunday would not only save many a man and woman from 'ruin' but would also produce better readers and thus better citizens. Having rested on Saturday night, 'let these minds clear and refreshed, have the Library on Sunday, and very few of them would be satisfied with "picture books"'.[87] While the focus of public libraries in the colonies was undoubtedly on the influence they could exert on young men, such libraries were increasingly viewed as important for members of both genders, and women's presence within their walls not only tolerated but encouraged.

Yet despite the increasing 'assertion' of 'their right to use the library', the presence of women could nonetheless be a distraction for men, and the unwanted attention of men could in turn discourage women from frequenting the library.[88] Richard Altick and Kate Flint have shown how the 'hordes of loungers' using British public libraries could 'not only put off potential women users ... but did not fit in with their administrators' impression about what formed a suitable environment for the female sex'.[89] Creating the *right* public space for women was therefore an important element in determining a public library's success. The lack of a ladies' room in the original MPL building prompted a discussion in the legislative council in 1858 and a number of letters from women swiftly appeared in the *Argus*, pointing to the necessity of a ladies' room to save women from the 'observation [of] many masculine eyes'.[90] One woman wrote that she did not 'possess [the] degree of courage' necessary to 'face the number of eyes which are raised, apparently in astonishment, when a lady makes her appearance in the present reading room, and which follow her every movement'.[91] Another writer directly confronted the disdainful characterisations of women who dared to 'infiltrate' the public library, arguing that women would require 'a separate room' until men did 'not consider a woman who reads anything more solid than poem or a novel as meddling with things that do not concern her' and as 'blue-stockings'.[92]

The gendering of reading spaces in the public library meant that these spaces themselves became coded by the types of reading associated with women. Examining the 'synopsis of the public library' provided in the 1861 MPL catalogue (Fig. 3.3), one can see that the area 'dedicated to ladies' is surrounded by categories of books such as 'Rural & Domestic Arts', 'Prose', 'Poetry', and 'Architecture & Art'. Unsurprisingly, *Melbourne Punch* played with the association of the ladies' room with frivolous activity and when a ban on eating in the room was enforced, the newspaper mocked the 'dear creatures! to be debarred from eating a bun, and even a bon-bon! … They may read about the Sandwich Islands, but not partake of a sandwich'.[93] Despite these jests at the expense of women users of the library, by 1871 the ladies' room appears to have grown significantly and is no longer placed in the 'light reading' section of the MPL. Rather tellingly, one of the walls of the room is now shared with the section dedicated to 'scientific societies transactions'.[94]

Indigenous and Non-British Readers

Indigenous subjects had very different rights across the British Empire, and their access to and engagement with colonial public libraries and other institutions of knowledge was similarly diverse. In Singapore, the education of the 'native population of the Colony' was a conspicuous part of the rhetoric surrounding the establishment of the RLM. While it was considered important that efforts should be made 'to convince the Native Princes and Rajaks of the policy of sending their sons to participate in the *benefits*' of the Singapore Institution Free School, the then Governor of the Straits Settlements, Andrew Clarke, proposed in 1874 that the RLM would itself be 'made the means of affording instruction not only to children, but to the adult population'.⁹⁵ Noting how different it was for British students, raised from birth with the principles of self-improvement and self-education, Robert Little, the future Chairman of the RLM, similarly argued in an address to the Singapore Legislative Council in 1874 that while the government was able to 'educate the native population of the Colony only up to a certain extent', they were nonetheless 'bound to do something to advance their education' after leaving school. Adopting a popular trope in nineteenth-century humanitarian discourse, Little drew comparisons between the Indigenous populations of the Straits and the poor of Britain and Europe when he argued that this 'could only be done by establishing libraries, "those vast armouries open to all indeed, but where the poor may always find their weapons"'.⁹⁶ He also noted that public libraries would have a positive effect on the crime rate associated with both European pauperism and Chinese and Malay communities, suggesting the extent to which the civilising mission directed at Indigenous populations shared many features with the 'paternalistic' approach to loaferism and other unacceptable forms of 'whiteness' discussed above.⁹⁷

Such arguments were, of course, also heavily bound up with the need to create a so-called comprador class of elite Indigenous and mixed-race civil servants in the colonial world. Little's desire to extend the role of Indigenous clerks from what he called 'mere copyists' to 'originators', who were able both to manage their own learning and to progress within the ranks of the civil service, was ultimately a means of encouraging Britishness. Yet it is significant that the proposed re-invigoration of Stamford Raffles's original vision for 'the cultivation of the languages of China, Siam, and Malay Archipelago, and the improvement of the moral and intellectual condition of the inhabitants of those countries', involved some sense of mutual exchange, not least because the library was, for the first time, to collect manuscripts and ethnographic works relating to the region, and to be united with a museum 'illustrating the products of the Malay Peninsula and Archipelago'.⁹⁸ The fact that at its opening in late 1874 the library had only attracted 102 subscribers out of a general population of over 96,000 people suggests that such lofty goals were hardly realised in practice.⁹⁹ While the 1877 RLM catalogue indicates that there was one Chinese member of the library governing committee and some wealthy Chinese and Malay subscribers, there is no available information on the extent to which 'native' populations visited the free reading room of the RLM.¹⁰⁰ There is also no detailed information in library reports on the nationalities of subscribers until 1904, at which point 72% of subscribers were British and 81% were

European (British, Dutch, German, etc.). The other 19% were predominantly Chinese. Even as late as 1922, the books in the library were mainly in English.[101]

Ambitions to educate the 'native' populations of Singapore, whether realised or not, were conspicuous by their absence in the establishment of public libraries in the South African and Australian colonies. In the Cape Colony, Indigenous literacy—and that of mixed-race *bastaard* and *griqua* communities—was primarily addressed by mission schools. Some mission stations such as Bethelsdorp, Genadendal, and Kat River had significant circulating libraries and relatively high English-language literacy levels among their primarily Khoisan communities,[102] but these stations in the Western and Eastern Cape were generally outside urban centres, and missionaries had little contact with the SAPL and its governing body. The 'Malay' ex-slave and Muslim community of Cape Town was served by its own networks of imams and madrasas.[103] The *Molteno Regulations* of 1874 technically allowed Indigenous and other non-white populations access to all reading rooms and reference material, but neither of these two groups was ever addressed either directly or indirectly by the SAPL. Put simply, they fell outside of the boundaries of who the SAPL committee members considered to be colonial citizenry. It was not until 1905 that F. S. Lewis, then Chief Librarian of the SAPL, could note that '[c]oloured people of all nationalities use these rooms, and one Malay is a subscriber'.[104]

In the Australian colonies, where Indigenous populations were in the minority by the mid-nineteenth century, there was little thought given to Indigenous literacy and education outside of mission schools and libraries, which were completely separated from the wider community.[105] Even in Singapore and Penang, where Indigenous and diasporic populations were in the majority, *laissez faire* attitudes towards the education of Indigenous populations, relatively high subscription fees, and the stocking of predominantly English or other European-language books meant that Indigenous investment in colonial libraries was limited to small groups of wealthy elites and the emerging literate middle classes. Public libraries, like other clubs and places of sociability, also acted as instruments of acculturation that were used to convey notions of Britishness both to British settlers and Indigenous elites. The social role of public libraries as places for lectures, classes, concerts, recitations, *conversaziones*, dances, and other recreational pursuits enhanced their function as bastions of 'whiteness' and middle-class social respectability. In this sense, public libraries, like other colonial clubs and associations, were the 'intellectual equivalent of the colonial "hill station", a place where colonists could go to rest and recuperate from the rigours of an alien environment'.[106] Despite their advocacy of free universal access, the cultural and social politics of colonial public libraries therefore contributed to, and even consolidated, the structures of colonial racism or what Stoler has called the 'private and public boundaries of race' well into the twentieth century.[107]

While the English-language emphasis of colonial public libraries corroborates to some extent James Belich's 'Anglo-divergence' model of the Anglophone settler revolution, European non-British readers, such as German and Dutch emigrants, fared somewhat better than Indigenous readers.[108] The SAI, for example, was prepared and even keen to cater for its German colonists, seeing itself as a 'national institution' for the 'education of the whole nation' rather than simply for the British contingent.[109] Ordering German titles was therefore a stated policy of the SAI, with committee notes recording the 'arrangements for the immediate importation of the best standard authors of Germany in the original language', supervised by 'resident German gentlemen'.[110] It was hoped that the German literature would become 'a prominent feature in the library' and 'be the means of increasing the number of German subscribers'.[111] Despite the high quality of the collection, the number of German titles held at the SAI was small: 53 titles of German literature out of approximately 4054 titles are listed in the SAI's 1861 catalogue. By 1869, 63 titles of German literature are listed out of approximately 6506 titles.[112] While German colonists had German-language newspapers, such as South Australia's short-lived *Deutsche Post* (est. 1848),[113] the SAI nonetheless recognised the importance of adapting their collection to the local needs and conditions of their colony, which was considered to be a defining characteristic of becoming a 'national' institution.

Apart from the partly Dutch-language Dessinian Collection of 4565 volumes, the SAPL also registered some desire to cater for the long-established Dutch population of the Cape. Of the 1584 titles listed in its 1829 catalogue, there are 157 Dutch titles in all genres, including natural history, voyages and travels, and ancient history.[114] While the library's Dutch-language holdings do not represent a large proportion of the SAPL's total holdings, they nonetheless amount to a numerically significant collection in comparison to the library's other foreign-language holdings (French, German, Italian, and Spanish), and reflect some effort to include the local Anglophile Cape-Dutch elite in the library. Yet by 1842, the Dutch-language works listed in the SAPL's catalogue amount to only

148 titles, suggesting that there was no ongoing desire to expand the library's Dutch holdings. On the contrary, by 1862, the number of Dutch titles listed is the reduced figure of 117.[115] While Jardine had maintained collections in Dutch, as well as collecting and preserving Cape print culture, it appears that his successor, Frederick Maskew, was more concerned with disseminating Anglophone literary and intellectual culture in a climate of increasingly intense Boer unrest and frontier warfare. Similarly, the SL made no attempt to stock books in any language other than English until its reincarnation as the RLM in 1874, despite the fact that Singapore was then a centre for commercial publishing in the Malay-Muslim world.[116]

At the SAPL's annual general meeting in 1855, a motion by the classicist and educationalist Dr Changuion bemoaned the lack of foreign-language literature in the library: 'all our annual accessions are exclusively in English. Now, sir, we ought to encourage the study of foreign languages and literature, as one of the means of promoting enlarged views'.[117] While Changuion ties the SAPL's emphasis on English-language books to parochialism or a resistance to the multi-lingual cosmopolitan cultures of continental Europe rather than to geo-political interests, Alistair Pennycook and Gauri Viswanathan, among others, have demonstrated how English-language instruction and education was used as part of a strategy to promote 'Britishness' in African, Asian, Indian, and West Indian colonies.[118] The book acquisition policies of public libraries in the southern colonies suggest a similarly close association between English-language book provision and geo-political interests, particularly in the Cape Colony and Singapore where there was a real material threat to Anglophone cultural hegemony due to the relatively small number of Anglo settlers as compared to other groups.

For colonies with negligible Dutch, French, and German populations, on the other hand, foreign-language collections were more a sign of cosmopolitanism and learnedness than of specific local needs. Although the majority of the works included in the 1861 MPL catalogue are in English and published in London, there are a variety of foreign-language titles listed, including titles in French, German, Italian, Latin, and Spanish. In 1884, C. W. Holgate reported of the MPL that its 'collection of works relating to the language, literature, and history of Germany' was the 'least well represented in proportion to its importance', but in the 1860s the literature section, in particular, demonstrates the library's wide-ranging selection of prestige texts and authors, with works in Greek, Latin, and modern languages such as French, Italian, German, Hungarian, and Russian.[119] Similarly, the TPL had a small classical and foreign-language collection, with its 1855 catalogue listing 31 French titles, 2 German titles, 19 Greek titles, and 20 Latin titles out of a total number of 2112 titles.[120] While foreign-language titles do not therefore amount to more than 3% of the TPL's collection, they nonetheless suggest a desire to encourage a cosmopolitan attitude among the library's users and, increasingly, to encourage the purchase and donation of antiquarian collections.

NOTES

1. Patrick Joyce, 'The Politics of the Liberal Archive', *History of the Human Sciences* 12, no. 3 (1999): 35–49 (39).
2. Michael Warner, *Publics and Counterpublics* (New York: Zone Books, 2002), 51, 81.
3. David Wittenberg, 'Going Out in Public: Visibility and Anonymity in Michael Warner's "Publics and Counterpublics"', *Quarterly Journal of Speech* 88, no. 4 (2002): 426–433 (426).
4. Ken Gelder and Rachael Weaver, *Colonial Australian Fiction: Character Types, Social Formations and the Colonial Economy* (Sydney: Sydney University Press, 2017), 1. Elizabeth Fowler, *Literary Character: The Human Figure in Early English Writing* (Ithaca NY: Cornell University Press, 2003), 2, quoted in Gelder and Weaver, 1.
5. *Proceedings*, SAPL, 1853, 6: www.ucd.ie/southhem/record.html#469.
6. *Sydney Morning Herald*, March 5, 1869, 3.
7. *Times* (London), October 16, 1841, 5.
8. *Sydney Morning Herald*, March 5, 1869, 3.
9. *The South Australian Institute: Comprising the Public Library, Art Gallery, and Museums. Addresses Delivered at the Laying of the Foundation* (Adelaide: W. K. Thomas & Co, 1879), 14.
10. Eric Richards, 'An Australian Map of British and Irish Literacy in 1841', *Population Studies* 53, no. 3 (1999): 345–359 (354, 353).
11. Malcolm Wood, *Australia's Secular Foundations* (Melbourne: Australian Scholarly Publishing, 2016), 66.
12. Kathleen Fennessy, *A People Learning: Colonial Victorians and their Public Museums* (Melbourne: Australian Scholarly Press, 2007), 16.
13. Johan Fourie, Robert Ross, and Russel Viljoen, 'Literacy at South African Mission Stations', *Journal of Southern African Studies* 40 (2014): 781–800.
14. J. E. Nathan, *The Census in British Malaya 1921* (London: Waterlow & Sons, 1922), 322, 332; James Francis Warren, *Rickshaw Coolie: A People's History of Singapore, 1880–1940* (Singapore: Singapore University Press, 2003), 45.
15. Ann L. Stoler, 'Rethinking Colonial Categories: European Communities and the Boundaries of Rule', *Comparative Studies in Society and History* 31, no. 1 (1989): 134–161 (150).

16. *Proceedings*, SAPL, 1848, 10, 13: www.ucd.ie/southhem/record.html#464.
17. *Proceedings of the Twenty-Sixth Anniversary Meeting of the Subscribers to the Public Library, Cape Town, Cape of Good Hope, Saturday, the 21st April, 1855* (Cape Town: Saul Solomon & Co., 1855), 2.
18. *Proceedings*, SAPL, 1853, 6: www.ucd.ie/southhem/record.html#469.
19. *The Third Report of the Singapore Library, 1847* (Singapore: G. M. Frederick at the Singapore Free Press Office, 1848), 4. For a list of subscribers, see *The Eighth Report of the Singapore Library, 1851* (Singapore: Mission Press, 1852), 3.
20. Ray Markey, 'Colonial Forms of Labour Organisation in Nineteenth-Century Australia' (Wollongong: Department of Economics Working Paper Series, University of Wollongong, 1997), 1–36, accessed August 2, 2018: http://ro.uow.edu.au/cgi/viewcontent.cgi?article=1261&context=commwkpapers.
21. Shayne Breen, 'Class', in *The Companion to Tasmanian History*, ed. Alison Alexander (Hobart: Centre for Tasmanian Historian Studies University of Tasmania, 2006), n. p., accessed August 3, 2018: http://www.utas.edu.au/library/companion_to_tasmanian_history/C/Class.htm.
22. *Herald* (Melbourne), May 27, 1861, 4.
23. *Age* (Melbourne), June 6, 1885 and *Australasian* (Melbourne), March, 1869, both quoted in David McVilly, '"Something to Blow About"?—the State Library of Victoria, 1856–1880', *La Trobe Journal* 8 (1971): 81–90 (83).
24. *Sydney Morning Herald*, May 22, 1878, 3.
25. *Mount Alexander Mail* (Castlemaine, Victoria), May 28, 1860, 3.
26. *Herald*, January 19, 1875, 2.
27. *Melbourne Punch*, August 25, 1859, 2; July 14, 1859, 3.
28. Lewis C. Roberts, 'Disciplining and Disinfecting Working-Class Readers in the Victorian Public Library', *Victorian Literature and Culture* 26, no. 1 (1998): 105–132 (120, 127).
29. Mary Hammond, '"The Great Fiction Bore": Free Libraries and the Construction of a Reading Public in England, 1880–1914', *Libraries & Culture* 37, no. 2 (Spring 2002): 83–108 (96, 86).
30. Mary Carroll and Sue Reynolds, '"There and Back Again": Reimagining the Public Library for the Twenty-First Century', *Library Trends* 62, no. 3 (2013): 581–595 (592).
31. *Melbourne Punch*, January 17, 1867, 3.
32. *Address on the Opening of The Free Public Library of Ballarat East by Sir Redmond Barry* (Ballarat: The Star Office, 1869), 11, 14.
33. Joyce, 'The Politics of the Liberal Archive', 41, 44.
34. *Argus* (Melbourne), April 10, 1863, 5.
35. *The First Report of the Singapore Library, 1844* (Singapore: Mission Press, 1845), 7.

36. Alistair Black, 'The People's University: Models of Public Library History', in *The Cambridge History of Libraries in Britain and Ireland Volume III 1640–1850*, ed. Giles Mandelbrote and K. A. Manley (Cambridge: Cambridge University Press, 2006), 24–39 (32); 'The Library as Clinic: A Foucauldian Interpretation of British Public Library Attitudes to Social and Physical Disease, ca. 1850–1950', *Libraries & Culture* 40, no. 3 (1995): 416–434 (426).
37. *South Australian Weekly Chronicle* (Adelaide), September 1, 1866, 4.
38. Black, 'The People's University', 32.
39. *Melbourne Punch*, May 19, 1864, 2.
40. *South Australian Weekly Chronicle*, October 31, 1863, 4.
41. Brendan Luyt, 'The Importance of Fiction to the Raffles Library, Singapore, During the Long Nineteenth-Century', *Library & Information History* 25, no. 2 (2009): 117–131.
42. Mrinalini Sinha, 'Britishness, Clubbability, and the Colonial Public Sphere: The Genealogy of an Imperial Institution in Colonial India', *Journal of British Studies* 40, no. 4 (2001): 489–52.
43. Marvin Spevack, 'The Impact of the British Museum Library', in *The Cambridge History of Libraries in Britain and Ireland Volume II 1640–1850*, ed. Giles Mandelbrote and K. A. Manley (Cambridge: Cambridge University Press, 2006), 422–437 (427). On this point, see *Melbourne Punch*, August 2, 1855, 153; and *Herald*, September 30, 1874, 2. See also *Herald*, March 28, 1862, 4; December 5, 1876, 2.
44. Hammond, '"The Great Fiction Bore"', 84.
45. *Melbourne Punch*, February 19, 1863, 4.
46. *Argus*, October 9, 1868, 5.
47. *Herald*, February 6, 1863, 5.
48. *North Australian* (Ipswich, Queensland), December 17, 1863, 7.
49. *Age*, February 18, 1856, 3.
50. *Age*, March 24, 1860, 4.
51. David McVilly, 'A History of the State Library of Victoria. 1853–1974' (MA thesis., Monash University, 1975), 38, accessed August 9, 2018: http://handle.slv.vic.gov.au/10381/231567.
52. McVilly, 'A History of the State Library of Victoria', 38.
53. *Argus*, October 9, 1868, 5.
54. *Empire* (Sydney), August 5, 1865, 5.
55. Michael Zakim, 'The Business Clerk as Social Revolutionary; or, a Labor History of the Nonproducing Classes', *Journal of the Early Republic* 26, no. 4 (Winter 2006): 563–603 (564).
56. Karl Marx, *Capital Vol. 1*, ed. Frederick Engels, trans. Samuel Moore and Richard Aveling (New York: International Publishers, 1967), 773–774.
57. *Age*, March 24, 1860, 4.

58. *Argus*, October 9, 1868, 5.
59. *Age*, March 24, 1860, 4.
60. *Herald*, January 29, 1863, 4.
61. *Melbourne Punch*, July 20, 1865, 6.
62. *South Australian Weekly Chronicle*, October 31, 1863, 4.
63. *Cape of Good Hope Literary Gazette*, June 29, 1831, 170.
64. *Herald*, September 7, 1869, 3.
65. *Melbourne Punch*, January 13, 1887, 3.
66. *Herald*, September 7, 1869, 3. On diseases in the public library see, for example, Hammond, '"The Great Fiction Bore"', 89.
67. Black, 'Library as Clinic', 416–434.
68. Harald Fischer-Tiné, 'Britain's Other Civilising Mission: Class Prejudice, European "Loaferism" and the Workhouse-system in Colonial India', *The Indian Economic and Social History Review* 42, no. 3 (2005): 295–338 (310, 330, 298).
69. *Sydney Morning Herald*, March 21, 1844, 2.
70. *Proceedings at the Twelfth Anniversary Meeting of Subscribers to the Public Library, Cape Town, Cape of Good Hope, Thursday, 29 April 1841* (Cape Town: s. n., 1841), 5.
71. *Melbourne Punch*, April 2, 1868, 4.
72. James Raven, 'Libraries for Sociability: The Advance of the Subscription Library', in *The Cambridge History of Libraries in Britain and Ireland Volume II 1640–1850*, ed. Giles Mandlebrote and K. A. Manley (Cambridge: Cambridge University Press, 2006), 239–263 (250).
73. *Catalogue*, ASL, 1839: http://www.ucd.ie/southhem/record.html#30. See also F. M. Bladen, *Public Library of New South Wales: Historical Notes*, 2nd ed. (Sydney: Govt. Printer, 1911), 27.
74. Heather Gaunt, 'Identity and Nation in the Australian Public Library: The Development of Local and National Collections 1850s–1940s, Using the Tasmanian Public Library as Case Study' (PhD diss., University of Tasmania, 2010), 53, accessed August 6, 2018: https://eprints.utas.edu.au/10772/2/Gaunt_whole.pdf. *The First Report of the Singapore Library, 1844* (Singapore: Mission Press, 1845), 2.
75. *Straits Times* (Singapore), April 24, 1875, 1.
76. *Proceedings at the Twenty-Ninth Anniversary Meeting of the Subscribers to the Public Library, Cape Town, Cape of Good Hope, Held on Saturday, The 1st May, 1858* (Cape Town: Saul Solomon, 1858), 14.
77. *Proceedings*, SAPL, 1853, 6: www.ucd.ie/southhem/record.html#469.
78. *Southern Australian* (Adelaide), August 28, 1840, 3.
79. Sarah Comyn, 'Literary Sociability on the Goldfields: The Mechanics' Institute in the Colony of Victoria, 1854–1870', *Journal of Victorian Culture* 23, no. 4 (2018): 447–462.
80. *South Australian Register* (Adelaide), May 13, 1856, 2.

81. *Mercury* (Hobart), August 21, 1860, 3; July 18, 1861, 2; July 11, 1862, 5; July 10, 1863, 2.
82. *Argus*, May 25, 1859, 6.
83. *Herald*, September 30, 1874, 2.
84. Roland Braddell, *The Lights of Singapore* (Oxford: Oxford University Press, 1982), 125.
85. *Argus*, July 13, 1859, 1.
86. *Sydney Morning Herald*, May 26, 1871, 5.
87. *Argus*, June 29, 1859, 5.
88. Abigail A. van Slyk, 'The Lady and the Library Loafer: Gender and Public Space in Victorian America', *Winterthur Portfolio* 31, no. 4 (Winter 1996): 221–242.
89. Kate Flint, *The Woman Reader, 1837–1914* (Oxford: Clarendon Press, 1993), 174; Richard Altick, *The English Common Reader: A Social History of the Mass Reading Public, 1800–1900* (Chicago: University of Chicago Press, 1957), 238.
90. *Age*, November 10, 1858, 5; *Argus*, November 19, 1851, 1.
91. *Argus*, November 19, 1858, 1.
92. *Argus*, November 25, 1858, 7.
93. *Melbourne Punch*, November 2, 1865, 3.
94. *Report of the Trustees of the Public Library, Museums, and National Gallery of Victoria, with the Reports of the Sectional Committees, for the Year 1870–71* (Melbourne: John Ferres, Government Printer, 1871), accessed August 9, 2018: https://www.parliament.vic.gov.au/vufind/Record/90063.
95. *Straits Times*, March 28, 1874, 1.
96. *Straits Observer*, December 18, 1874, 2; *Straits Times*, December 26, 1874, 4.
97. Fischer-Tiné, 'Britain's Other Civilising Mission', 298.
98. *Straits Times*, March 28, 1874, 1.
99. *Report on the Raffles Library and Museum for the Year 1875* (Singapore: Government Printing Office, 1876), 1. For the population of Singapore in 1871, see Saw Swee-Hock, 'Population Trends in Singapore, 1819–1967', *Journal of South Asian History* 10, no. 1 (1969): 36–49 (39).
100. *General Catalogue of Bound Works in the Raffles Library, Sept. 1st 1877*, n.p., accessed August 4, 2018: http://eservice.nlb.gov.sg/data2/BookSG/publish/c/c70105a0-39a8-4ea2-9d99-22dcdb23d62a/web/html5/index.html?opf=tablet/BOOKSG.xml&launchlogo=tablet/BOOKSG_BrandingLogo_.png.
101. Lim Peng Han, 'The Beginning and Development of the Raffles Library in Singapore, 1823–1941: A Nineteenth-Century and Early Twentieth-Century British Colonial Enclave', *Library and Information History* 25, no. 4 (2009): 265–278 (270).

102. J. Sales, *Mission Stations and the Coloured Communities of the Eastern Cape, 1800–1852* (Cape Town and Rotterdam: A. A. Balkema, 1975), 43.
103. Saarah Jappie, 'Jawi Dari Jauh: 'Malays' in South Africa Through Text', *Indonesia and the Malay World* 40 (2012): 143–159; Achmat Davids, *The Afrikaans of the Cape Muslims from 1805 to 1915*, ed. Hein Willems and Suleman E. Dangor (Pretoria: Protean Book House, 2011).
104. F. S. Lewis, 'Memorandum to B. Dyer', April 17, 1905, quoted in Marguerite Andree Peters, 'The Contribution of the (Carnegie) Non-European Library Service, Transvaal, to the Development of Library Services for Africans in South Africa' (PhD diss., University of Cape Town, 1974), 23, accessed August 3, 2018: https://open.uct.ac.za/bitstream/handle/11427/14799/thesis_hum_1974_peters_marguerite_andra_copy_e.pdf?sequence=1.
105. See, for example, Ian D. Clark, *'A Peep at the Blacks': A History of Tourism at Coranderrk Aboriginal Station, 1863–1924* (Warsaw and Berlin: De Gruyter, 2015).
106. Luyt, 'The Importance of Fiction', 123.
107. Ann L. Stoler, 'Making Empire Respectable: The Politics of Race and Sexual Morality in twentieth-Century Colonial Cultures', *American Ethnologist* 16, no. 4 (1989): 634–660 (635).
108. James Belich, *Replenishing the Earth: The Settler Revolution and the Rise of the Anglo-World, 1783–1939* (Oxford: Oxford University Press, 2009), 111.
109. *South Australian Register*, October 18, 1859, 5.
110. *Adelaide Times*, October 6, 1857, 3; *Adelaide Observer*, May 1, 1858, 3.
111. *South Australian Register*, October 18, 1859, 5.
112. *Catalogue*, SAI, 1861: http://www.ucd.ie/southhem/record.html#113; *Catalogue*, SAI, 1869: http://www.ucd.ie/southhem/record.html#188.
113. H. C. Weibgen, *Catalog der Bibliothek/Bendigo Deautscher Verein und Lesehalle* (Sandhurst, Vic: C. Jones & Co, 1874). For German-language libraries in Victoria, see Wallace Kirsop, 'Bendigo's Nineteenth-Century German Library', *Bulletin (Bibliographical Society of Australia and New Zealand)* 18, no. 2–3 (1994): 169–172.
114. *Catalogue*, SAPL, 1829: http://www.ucd.ie/southhem/record.html#264.
115. *Catalogue*, SAPL, 1842: http://www.ucd.ie/southhem/record.html#269; *Catalogue*, SAPL, 1862: http://www.ucd.ie/southhem/record.html#270.
116. C. M. Turnbull, *A History of Modern Singapore, 1819–2005* (Singapore: NUS Press, 2009), 111.
117. *Proceedings of the Twenty-Sixth Anniversary Meeting of the Subscribers to the Public Library, Cape Town … 1855*, 12–13.
118. Alistair Pennycook, *English and the Discourses of Colonialism* (London and New York: Routledge 1998); Gauri Viswanathwan, *Masks of Conquest: Literary Study and British Rule in India* (New York: Columbia University Press, 1989).

119. *Catalogue*, MPL, 1861: http://www.ucd.ie/southhem/record.html#112. C. W. Holgate, *An Account of the Chief Libraries of Australia and Tasmania* London: Chiswick, Press, 1886), quoted in Wallace Kirsop, 'German Science in Nineteenth-Century Australian Libraries', *The Royal Society of Victoria* 127 (2015): 39–42 (39).
120. *Catalogue*, TPL, 1855: http://www.ucd.ie/southhem/record.html#312.

Open Access This chapter is licensed under the terms of the Creative Commons Attribution 4.0 International License (http://creativecommons.org/licenses/by/4.0/), which permits use, sharing, adaptation, distribution and reproduction in any medium or format, as long as you give appropriate credit to the original author(s) and the source, provide a link to the Creative Commons licence and indicate if changes were made.

The images or other third party material in this chapter are included in the chapter's Creative Commons licence, unless indicated otherwise in a credit line to the material. If material is not included in the chapter's Creative Commons licence and your intended use is not permitted by statutory regulation or exceeds the permitted use, you will need to obtain permission directly from the copyright holder.

CHAPTER 4

'A mob of light readers': Holdings, Genre Proportions, and Modes of Reading

Abstract This chapter examines the genre proportions of public library collections in the southern colonies, arguing that they both reflect and are a response to debates about the 'fiction problem', modes of reading, local colonial conditions, and the utility of public libraries. Along with its analysis of changing genre proportions, the chapter also explores the symbolic and educational power of the library catalogue in facilitating the public library's role as a national institution and as a means of fostering transnational intellectual and print networks.

Keywords Light reading • The 'fiction problem' • Library holdings • Bequests • Catalogues

Following a debate about the wisdom of introducing a new (third) class of subscribers to the SAPL at its committee's 1848 annual meeting, the Attorney General, William Porter, made a gendered comparison between a taste for the latest literature and the pursuit of fashion:

> as to the right of first perusal, there are some gentlemen—not the wisest, perhaps—who look with as much contempt on last year's book, as some ladies—not, perhaps, the wisest either—do on last year's bonnet.[1]

Although the committee members were committed to providing that 'first blessing of life—HOME EDUCATION', they were not ignorant of the pecuniary benefits attached to the provision of fashionable literature.[2] Porter's jesting point was that first- and second-class subscribers would be willing to pay more to have priority access to the newest additions to the library. In a characterisation reminiscent of 'Lavinia Readmuch' of Chap. 3, Porter portrays the pursuit of novelty in reading as not only unwise, but also as analogous to the faddish behaviour of women: books are read and discarded with as little considered interest as the latest fashion accessories. A year later his fellow committee member, Reverend Newman, used stronger terms to warn against reading the 'fashionable novel', describing them as 'unworthy [of] the mature mind' and encouraging 'a dissatisfaction of ordinary, every-day life, with which most of us have to do'. Arguing that such fiction was, at best, a distraction for young men that led them to 'lay aside all studious and useful and refined reading' and, at worst, a practice that could 'diffuse atheism, anarchic violence, contempt for … decency and order', Newman suggested that fiction holdings should be severely curtailed.[3]

Although—or perhaps because—it provided free access to its reference-only collections, the MPL similarly looked upon fashionable works of 'purely ephemeral description and of transient value' with disdain and 'set [them] aside for those which commend[ed] themselves for their substantial merit and sterling value'.[4] This tension between ephemeral works and those of 'permanent merit' dominated debates about the libraries' collections, the proportions of various genres contained therein, and the purpose they served in the southern colonies. Central to the fixation on the proportion of fiction relative to other genres was a belief that libraries could be used for the moral improvement of society. Lewis C. Roberts notes, in the British context, that following the 1849 Select Committee on Public Libraries a shift occurred from the '"softening and expanding influences" of reading to the "instrumentality of well-chosen books"'. Library committees' careful selection of fictional works was therefore part of a process not only of educating library users but of disciplining readers (see Chap. 3), particularly the working classes for whom 'fiction remained the only kind of text they could, and would ever want, to read'.[5]

While the period of our study is characterised by a general concern about novel reading across Europe and North America, this chapter demonstrates how libraries in the southern colonies both addressed and participated in these debates, and used the content of their collections to respond to local conditions, thereby establishing and defending their purpose as 'national' institutions. During a 'Special General meeting of the Proprietors' of the ASL convened by the Presbyterian cleric John Dunmore Lang in 1844, the latter denounced the library's holdings as consisting of the 'merest trash—novels and romances, exceeding in proportion works of useful and sterling merit, to a greater extent than he recollected ever to have witnessed in any such an institution', and questioned how the collection would 'evoke the intellect [or] raise the character of the colony'. In a pre-planned response, the library committee defended the quality of the library and pointed to the broad range of the collection, which was reported to contain 'upwards of two thousand works on biography and history, an ample supply of works on geography, on all the sciences, also of classics, and of English standard works of every description'. In support of the number of novels contained in the library, the Congregational minister and ASL committee member Robert Ross argued that while he, himself, 'did not advocate this description of reading', he thought the proportion of novels was 'not at all too large' for an institution 'which had for its object the convenience of members'.[6]

Reverend James Adamson, leader of the St. Andrew's Scottish Church in Cape Town, adopted a similar tone in defence of novels during the 1848 annual meeting of subscribers at the SAPL. While acknowledging that it is 'our duty to increase, as it is in our power, the number of works of learning and science', he also noted that 'I am not against the introduction of the lighter literature of the age, called novels'.[7] Advocate William Musgrave, also of the SAPL Committee, had already argued in 1841 that it is not 'everyone who reads merely for the sake of being edified', necessitating that 'an Institution of this description' unite 'instruction with the recreation of the mind'. Celebrating the 'mixed character' of the works in the SAPL collection, Musgrave concluded that 'while they form so delightful a resource to us in our leisure hours, [they] never fail to mingle with their enchantment something like a moral lesson to the reader'.[8]

Ross, Musgrave, and Adamson's qualified support of the number of novels contained in the ASL and SAPL points to an ongoing anxiety about whether the genre proportions of their collections reflected the purpose—actual or ideal—of the library as a public institution. The potential conflicts between a library's purpose and the content and use of its collections were not, of course, confined to the libraries of the southern colonies. While James Hole, author of the 1853 *An Essay on the History and Management of Literary, Scientific, & Mechanics' Institutions*, argued that the total 'exclusion [of fiction] appears to us indefensible', he lamented the 'disproportion' of fiction collections and complained that despite the careful selection of books at the Leeds Institute 'the fiction and periodical literature is much more than half the circulation!'.[9] Martin Lyons notes that 'popular practices' in France similarly 'failed to conform to the norms of librarians. In the 1880s and 1890s, more than half the borrowings from Parisian municipal libraries was of novels'.[10]

Christine Pawley's study of libraries in nineteenth-century North America usefully identifies three categories of response to the 'fiction problem': the 'small minority call[ing] for total abstinence', the reluctant tolerators, and finally those who promoted the reading of fiction because 'any reading … was better than none at all, especially if it encouraged people to progress up the literary ladder'.[11] Pawley's metaphor of a 'literary ladder' up which readers could possibly ascend, beginning with novels as the first wrung, echoes a stadial theory of reading present in discussions surrounding the genre proportions of colonial public libraries. Lamenting the 'great mischief' done by certain types of novels—'Oliver Twist and Jack Shepherd' and 'the sentimentality of Rousseau', for example—during his 1857 address, the Anglican Bishop and educator Canon White identifies three types of reading of which the 'lowest style' is reading for 'horror and laughter'. Readers of this style need to be encouraged to 'absorb' a different 'literary nutriment' that is 'high and noble and pure in life and character'. In contrast to the 'habit of reading satirical and ludicrous works alone', White argues that readers of poetry—and the occasional Walter Scott novel—are seekers of beauty and represent a 'second class of readers'. The 'attainment of truth' is identified by White as the third and highest class of reading, to which all should aspire, and includes the genres of science, history, and philosophy.[12]

Crucially, in his account of 'reading for beauty', White argues that poetry needs to be all the more celebrated because the 'other arts' of a similar class, such as 'music, painting, architecture', are not sufficiently developed in the colony to encourage the improvement of the mind:

> instead of lamenting over the absence of what we have not, the public mind of a colony ought to be more carefully directed to poetry, which it can possess in perfection, because it lacks a full measure of kindred arts, which, in other lands, help in their measure to train and develop similar faculties of the soul.[13]

White's recognition of the local conditions that must of necessity shape the colony's library collection was shared by the SL's management committee, who explicitly focused their attention on collecting light fiction: 'since the general object of the majority of subscribers in seeking the Library will be to procure a pleasant relaxation from their business, care will be taken that the contents of a large division of the shelves shall serve for light reading'.[14] In a mercantile environment such as Singapore, entertainment was viewed as an important function of the library. As Brendan Luyt has argued, 'boredom was a constant fact of life for colonialists' and reading, even of light fiction, was seen as providing relief and occupation.[15]

The genre proportions of the SL's 1860 catalogue reflect the acceptance of 'light reading' as a means of meeting the needs of the community, with 'Imaginative Literature' making up 44% of the collection (Appendix C, Table C.1). 'Biography and History' is the next highest represented category at 31%. The SL was not alone in recognising the ameliorative potential of fiction, drama, and poetry. Between 1860 and 1862, the SAI's holdings contained 37% 'Imaginative Literature', and while the SAPL held less 'Imaginative Literature' comparatively with 17%, it is still the third highest category in its collection (Appendix C, Tables C.2 and C.3). It is perhaps not so surprising, then, that in the same year Canon White was warning against the negative effects of novel reading in the Cape Colony, the Attorney General of South Australia, Richard Hanson, provided an emphatic defence of the novel at the first public meeting of the SAI, arguing that 'novel reading is on the whole of a beneficial tendency' and that 'as a source of pleasure merely, apart from the lessons it may impart and the tendencies it may foster, literature is well worthy of our encouragement'. Emphasising the potential of the novel to play a positive role in political change, he pointed to the example of Harriet Beecher Stowe's *Uncle Tom's Cabin* (1852), which he believed had provided the 'most eloquent and effectual appeal against the atrocities of negro slavery in the United States'.[16]

The MPL, in contrast, actively resisted the trend of accepting 'lighter' literature onto its shelves as unworthy of its status as a 'national institution'. But while the MPL prided itself on being the standard-bearer of a public library in the southern colonies, its adherence to the reference library model received criticism from other colonies for not addressing local needs and desires. An article in the *Tasmanian Times* in 1868 discussing the need for a public library in Hobart explicitly rejected the MPL model. The rationale for this rejection was not only because the *Times* viewed a freely circulating library as a *truly* public model, but also because it argued that the MPL did not address the need for rational recreation and family reading:

'Such a library is not in any demand here. We can get on very well in the meantime without such a resort for novel-readers, idle apprentices, "discarded tapsters and unjust servingmen" as the Melbourne Public Library is well known to be'. The writer instead argues that the people of Hobart prefer to read in family or domestic settings such as 'their firesides and would be rarely indeed found in the Town Hall'. Concluding that 'what is urgently wanted, is a good library from which people can get for themselves and for their families an abundant supply of attractive and wholesome literature', the writer proposes a combination of a circulation and a reference library, arguing that 'a grand library for consultation is out of the question here'.[17]

If these kinds of arguments coincided with the rise of reading as a leisure activity for both the literate middle and working classes, as well as pointing to an acknowledgment of the particular need for wholesome leisure in the colonies—a need repeated in the debates surrounding all of our colonial libraries—they are also suggestive of the specificity of each colony's response to that need according to local conditions. While a vague blueprint for 'public-library-making' seemed to exist, the most important element for success was adaptability.[18] Examining the libraries' collections provides an opportunity to identify the local conditions that shaped the libraries' collections, the inventive ways libraries chose to respond to these demands, and the commonalities and distinctiveness of their experiences in developing and maintaining their status as public and national institutions.

Public Funding v. User-Pays Subscription Models

The SAPL's conversion from a public to a subscription library, following the withdrawal of public funding in 1829, is detectable in the genre proportions of the library's holdings. Between 1825 and 1829, the proportion of 'Imaginative Literature' dropped from 11% to 4% while the proportion of 'Science' rose from 6% to 21% (Appendix C, Table C.3). A supplementary catalogue from 1826 illustrates this growth in the 'Science' category and demonstrates the SAPL's dedication to forming a prestige scientific reference collection with 146 scientific titles added to the collection.[19] After 1829 and the introduction of a subscription fee, there was a steady rise in 'Imaginative Literature' accompanied by a reduction in the proportions of 'Science', and of 'Political Economy, Politics, and Jurisprudence'. By 1862 the best represented categories are 'Biography and History' (29%), 'Geography, Voyages, and Travel' (18%), and 'Imaginative Literature' (17%) (Appendix C, Table C.3).

Despite its change in funding and priorities, the SAPL remained committed to the continued status of its reference collection, realising that as an institution of knowledge it had an important role to play in the Cape Colony's efforts to achieve a representative government. Attaining a representative assembly required, according to Attorney General Porter, the 'young men of the Colony' to be educated, to 'meditate upon the principles of public business', and to 'store [their minds] with political knowledge'.[20] While fiction could be tolerated to meet the desires of subscribers, it could not be allowed to overshadow the rest of the collection. In response, the library developed innovative ways to manage the demand for fiction from its subscribers, as shall be seen in the discussion of the circulating library below.

The SAPL was, however, an unusual case. In the southern colonies, it was more common for public libraries to succeed subscription libraries. This was the case in Singapore with the transformation from the SL, a proprietary subscription library, to the RLM in 1874. The RLM was divided into three sections: a reference section open to the public; a lending section, with borrowing available only to subscribers (with various classes of subscription rights); and a free reading room available to all users.[21] The move to partial public funding saw a reduction in the proportion of 'Imaginative Literature' from 36% in 1863 to 28% in 1877 (Appendix C, Table C.1), but Robert Little, Chairman of the RLM management committee, continued to advocate for the benefits of entertaining reading. Addressing the Legislative Council in 1874, Little argued that the public library would benefit 'native' education and protect European youth against the dangers of the 'gaming table', providing 'one "of the greatest safeguards we could find for the young people of the Settlement"'. Responding to criticism of 'spending public funds in the purchase of novels for young ladies to read', Little noted that as the 'Premier himself was a writer of novels it would not be becoming to say anything against novel reading'.[22] Dr Little did concede, however, that the 'reference library was intended for a higher class than would use the lending one', reflecting the class-inflected discourses discussed in the previous chapter.[23] The division between the public and subscription sections of the library would overshadow discussions of the RLM's perceived purpose and value throughout its early history.

The mixed function of the SAI, as both mechanics' institute and subscription library, meant that the library was dogged by discussions about whether it was a public or a private institution, and how effectively the library served either purpose. During its existence as the SALMI (1848–1856) the library was unique in receiving some government aid towards buying books. Significant tension was, however, created between the mechanics' institute and the library, with many letters to the editor complaining that the mechanics' institute had lost its original purpose through its amalgamation with the library, and that funds that should have been dedicated to classes and lectures for the working classes were diverted to books for the library: 'The energy of the working men has been paralysed by the inertia of the Library drones'.[24] The criticisms levelled against the collection for being 'a mere reading club and lending library of many trashy novels, in fact a cheap substitute for, and rival to, Mr. Platt's shop' is the result of a dramatic rise in the proportion of imaginative literature.[25] Between 1848 and 1851, 'Imaginative Literature' increased from 16% to 36% of the collection, a significant rise that effected a proportionate decrease in all other genres, the most significant being a drop from 15% to 8% in 'Science' (Appendix C, Table C.2). Given the commitment of the mechanics' institute to 'train the youth of the colony', it is not surprising that they responded with dismay to the substitution of literature for science.[26]

Upon becoming part of the SAI in 1856, the library offered a similar mix of public/private funding and access to that of the RLM. Although the proportion of 'Imaginative Literature' saw a slight increase from 36% in 1851 to 37% in 1861, it had dropped to 27% by 1869, whereas all other categories increased or remained stable (Appendix C, Table C.2). Books could only be borrowed on payment of a membership fee and, as with the RLM, this concomitant public/private funding was to dominate debates about the library's purpose and its circulation figures. It also explains the persistence of 'Imaginative Literature' at such a high proportion of the collection. As Priya Joshi has argued in the context of nineteenth-century public libraries in India, 'the persistence of the fiction holdings … as evidenced in their reports and catalogues makes clear' that the institutions were not easily able 'to change matters: readers, it seemed, exercised a considerable voice over what they wanted to read, and the libraries were more or less forced to oblige or to risk losing members'.[27]

As the controversy ignited by J. D. Lang at the ASL indicates, 'Imaginative Literature' formed a significant proportion of the ASL's genre proportions, reaching its highest points at 30% in the 1843 catalogue and 33% in the 1845 supplementary catalogue, after which it saw a decrease before again dominating the collection in 1853 at 28% (the second largest category being 'Biography and History' at 21%) (Appendix C, Table C.4). The impact of the transferal of the ASL collection to the FPL in 1869 is clear in the heavily annotated and marked-up *List of the Books in the Free Public Library* (1869), which demonstrates the extent to which novels were expunged from the collection.[28] During his address at the opening of the FPL in 1869, Somerset Richard Lowry-Corry, the Earl of Belmore and Governor of New South Wales, alluded to the fact that objectionable books—primarily fiction—were being removed from the collection: 'it is the intention of the Government to remove from the institution such books as it may be undesirable to retain in a free library and to purchase at once in the colony additional works of a suitable kind'.[29] Later catalogues of the FPL show that only a select number of the works of approved novelists were retained in the collection, and these works of prose fiction were not available for borrowing.[30]

The TPL's imaginative literature holdings in the 1850s reflect the elitist nature of the library in its earliest incarnation as a subscription library that was 'unashamedly middle class with upper class pretensions'.[31] The purchase of Colonial Secretary James Ebenezer Bicheno's collection of 2500 books for the special price of £300 following his death in 1851 had a significant impact on genre proportions and reflects the Trustees' desire to establish a serious collection at the TPL from its foundation.[32] The proportions of 'Imaginative Literature' are significantly lower than for the ASL, for example, 12% in 1852 with a slight increase to 16% in 1855. While the TPL may have resisted the demand for imaginative literature in the 1850s, its collection reflects the popularity of another genre of the period: 'Geography, Voyages, and Travel' saw the largest increase from 12% (1852) to 22% (1855), whereas 'Biography and History' declined from 28% to 21%. 'Science' remained the same at 13% (Appendix C, Table C.5).

The fact that the MPL was publicly and generously funded with an initial building grant of £10,000 plus £3000 for books sets it apart from those libraries that had their origins as subscription libraries.[33] Between 1853 and 1861, the MPL spent £25,785 on purchasing books and by 1869 had spent £47,535 of the very substantial £53,750 voted by parliament towards its book fund.[34] The 1861 catalogue explicitly ties the government's endorsement to the prestige and purpose of the collection, stating that Governor La Trobe was 'fully impressed with the importance of the influence likely to arise from voluntary adult mental improvement, as well as of the intellectual and moral elevation to be created by a cultivation of the works of standard authors'.[35] In his first order to the colonial agent Edward Barnard, Redmond Barry specified that the books chosen for the MPL needed to be 'the best Editions', defined as 'the latest, most carefully edited, collated and illustrated by notes or otherwise, not such as recommend themselves solely by being gaudily bound'. Barry further specified that 'works of ephemeral character be avoided unless especially named'.[36] Barry's instructions to Barnard are explicitly tied to his understanding of the MPL as not only a library open and free to the public, but also as an institution contributing to the status of the colony of Victoria. This view of the MPL as both a *national* institution and an international emissary for the colony as a whole is equally evident in the Trustees' Report of 1870–1871, which includes a comparison of the volumes of the MPL's holdings, access hours and conditions, and number of visitors with free libraries in Britain, North America, France, Germany, and Italy.[37]

The 1854 catalogue for the first consignment of books sent by the MPL's London supplier, J. J. Guillaume, is indicative of Barry's ambition to cultivate 'intellectual and moral elevation' by stocking 'works by standard authors'.[38] Non-fiction titles occupy most of the collection with the (original MPL) categories of science, history, and philosophy well represented, and a significant presence of periodicals (608 volumes in total). While poetry forms a considerable part of the MPL's literature category, few novels are listed, and all are by men. Very few women writers appear in this catalogue and their contribution is limited to memoirs of royalty and a translated history by Sarah Austin.[39] Unlike public libraries that retained the user-pays model where romances by female writers were in great demand—and not just by women—the MPL could afford to take a hard line against the imaginative literature it viewed as undesirable. Whereas the SL's best-represented imaginative writers in 1863 included women writers such as Catherine Gore (12 titles), Frances Trollope (10 titles), and Margaret Oliphant (8 titles),[40] the MPL's 1861 catalogue shows it confined its interest in imaginative writing by women to more instructive and edifying authors such as Charlotte Brontë (4 titles) and Maria Edgeworth (2 titles).[41] By contrast the MPL listed 17 titles by the female art historian Anna Jameson.

'Biography and History' dominate the 1861 MPL catalogue, forming 31% of the collection (Appendix C, Table C.6). Although comparatively less than the 'Biography and History' holdings, scientific works still form a sizeable portion at 12% of the collection. The collection of classical works in Greek and Latin and its wide-ranging selection of works in modern languages—such as Dutch, French, Italian, German, Hungarian, and Russian—demonstrates the MPL's commitment to selecting prestige texts and authors. Donations received from foreign governments in the 1860s—for example, from the government of the Netherlands—further contributed to the MPL's relatively strong collection of foreign-language titles.[42] The MPL's impressive collection of foreign-language Bibles was the result of a significant donation by the British and Foreign Bible Society.[43] *Belles lettres* and critical works formed a substantial part of the library's literature category. When critical works are excluded, however, 'Imaginative Literature' forms a significantly smaller portion of the MPL's collection in comparison to the other colonial libraries already examined at only 5%, demonstrating that between 1854 and 1861, during which time the MPL grew its collection from 3846 to 26,723 volumes, the Trustees remained steadfast in their commitment to 'standard authors' (Appendix C, Table C.6).[44]

Responding to Demands for Circulation

While the MPL did not operate a circulating library until 1890, it did offer a 'travelling libraries' scheme from 1860, sending cases of books to other libraries (mainly mechanics' institutes) within a ten-mile radius of Melbourne.[45] Responding to what the Melbourne *Herald* called the 'reproach of "centralisation"' directed at the MPL by country and provincial institutions, the Trustees' Report of 1870–1871 shows that the scheme was not immune to the demands for fiction and *belles lettres*, with 'British Literature' making up 28% of the volumes circulated as opposed to 14% for 'Geography and Travels', and 13% for 'British History', the second and third highest categories respectively.[46] The SAI also adopted a scheme of lending books to affiliated mechanics' institutes, with 54 country institutes affiliated by 1869. This scheme continued until the 1890s, and by 1895 there were 154 participating institutes with 199 boxes of books and 6545 books in circulation.[47]

The challenge posed by the demand for fiction was naturally more deeply felt by those libraries dependent on subscriptions for funding. Responding to the criticism in 1861 that the SAI contained too many novels for a public library, the South Australian Chief Justice, Sir Charles Cooper, agreed but argued that if novels 'are fit to be read they must form a part of every public library on a considerable scale'.[48] Although we have no borrowing statistics according to genre for the SAI, anecdotal evidence from the annual reports points to the popularity of novels, with a Mr. Barnard claiming that the 'simplest and readiest way of ascertaining what works were read was by noticing that state of the covers of the book'. Assessing the material condition of the books, Barnard could confidently state that 'the more popular books—not the works of Dickens and Thackeray only—but those of

Macaulay, give evidence of frequent perusal'.[49] Like the Tasmanian commentator who saw the need for public libraries to allow lending so that families could read together in domestic settings, commentators in South Australia agreed that the circulating library both contributed funds to the institute and 'encourag[ed] family reading', but that the disadvantages, including the permanent damage to books, 'may render it necessary to discontinue the circulating system'.[50] The frustration with the effect the circulating library was having on the SAI's role as a public and reference institution persisted until the SAI was replaced by the Public Library, Museum and Gallery in 1884, whereupon the subscription library was finally separated to become the Adelaide Circulating Library.

The long-serving SAPL librarian Alexander Jardine responded to the threat he saw subscriber demands posing to the composition and status of the library collection by developing an annotated catalogue of instruction. The 1842 SAPL catalogue contains detailed bibliographic commentary through which Jardine directs readers to what he viewed as the most authoritative texts in each of the library's 44 subject classes. In the footnotes accompanying the 'Imaginative works' class, Jardine cites a range of eminent scientific and literary sources including Francis Bacon, Thomas Gray, and William Cowper. While allowing that 'the severer judgment of [Samuel] *Johnson* was unwilling to abandon the pleasant aid of romance as part of education', Jardine advises that 'these authorities should not be used to encourage a passion of continuous novel reading. A walk in the garden is both pleasant and salutary; but it is not desirable to live in it'. Jardine concludes his warning against novels with a quote from Southey: 'Of novels as they swarm from the modern press, I have no hesitation in saying, that many are poisonous and few are of any use'.[51]

Despite Jardine's efforts to protect the SAPL's reputation as a serious research institution from the dangers of novel reading, the anxiety evident in Canon White's 1857 address points to the persistence of subscribers' demands for fiction. White's criticism of novel readers was due, in part, to the significant portion of novels being borrowed in comparison with history and the sciences. White's breakdown of borrowings ranked from highest to lowest is as follows: 'Novels' 55%; 'Voyages and Travels' 16%; 'Biography' 8%; 'Miscellaneous' 8%; 'History' 7%; 'Arts and Sciences' 3%; 'Politics, Law and Economics' 3%; and 'Poetry' 1%.[52] Luyt's analysis of the acquisition and borrowing records of the RLM similarly shows that fiction continued to form an important part of its collection despite its being partially publicly funded. For example, 34% of the acquisitions for 1886 were works of fiction and the circulation figures point to an increasing demand for fiction from 70% of the circulation in 1881 to 87% in 1905.[53] While Jardine's advisory annotations did not curb the enthusiasm for fiction, his strategy of using the library catalogue to educate its users and cultivate 'correct' literary taste anticipated the strategies of librarians in Britain. Antonio Panizzi employed a similar method in his *British Museum: A Short Guide to that Portion of the Library of Printed Books Now Open to the Public* (1851).[54]

Cultivating Taste and Modes of Reading

The perception of library committees that public libraries were educators and taste-makers within their colonies is evident in their repeated use of the metaphor of cultivation. When discussing the reading habits of the SAI patrons, Justice Cooper reminded his audience that 'various plants require various modes of cultivation, and that a taste for reading is a plant of delicate growth, which will not admit of being forced'.[55] Even Canon White, who was generally dismissive of the novel's potential benefits, turned to the trope of cultivation in his address to the SAPL, admitting that 'it is a narrow and unwholesome view of the use of literature, which condemns the use of that wonderful faculty, imagination ... I believe that the imagination requires to be cultivated as the other faculties do, in order to preserve the proper harmony of man's inner nature; and like them it must be guided and regulated'.[56] The MPL, too, described its role in these terms. The 1870–1871 Trustees' Report introduces a comparison of the MPL's 'literary resources' to those of other colonies with a call for their 'fellow-countrymen' to 'recognize the truths enforced by the history of the ages that the greatest dangers to freedom arise from the prevalence of ignorance and vice, and that provision must be made for the cultivation and expansion of the public mind, according as it becomes charged with the exercise of political privileges'.[57]

The report's reference to 'political privileges' points to the colony of Victoria's significant achievement of responsible government in 1854, but also has clear parallels with the earlier arguments made at the SAPL that public libraries had an important role to play in educating members of the colonies in how to responsibly participate in civic and political life (see Chap. 2). The SAI's governing committee evidently shared this sentiment. In an address to mark the publication of the library's 1861 catalogue, Sir Charles Cooper reiterated the connection between political privileges, responsibility, and the importance of the library as provider of knowledge, noting that whereas in England 'a man born in poverty must climb a weary height before he reaches the gate of entrance to political life', in South Australia 'every man of ordinary energy on attaining his full manhood has privileges' that it is his 'duty to exercise', stressing the need for 'sound knowledge' in carrying out these political duties.[58]

Cognisant of the social, cultural, and political significance of their roles in the colonies, these libraries aimed not only to cultivate a taste for particular types of content, but also to develop particular modes of reading. Anxious about 'surface' readers who read only what was fashionable and who were attracted by the covers of books rather than their content, the MPL Trustees repeatedly attacked books of 'a purely ephemeral description and of transient value', setting them 'aside' for those of permanent merit. The MPL instead defined and defended the character of its collection by pointing to the relative absence of 'works usually classed as works of fiction and of the imagination, and those which in some catalogues are entered under the head of "literature for juveniles"'.[59] Such was Redmond Barry's disdain for novels that he is reported as having celebrated the theft of them from the MPL.[60]

While the MPL was the most vociferous in its condemnation of the 'ephemera' that would never encourage serious reading, surface reading was a concern shared by all the libraries and accompanied the push for collections that reflected their status as 'permanent' institutions. The *Straits Times* criticised the SL, for example, because the collection was 'designed for present reading, and consequently partaking more of the light character as novels, magazines, reviews and other ephemeral emanations from the press: works of a purely scientific character are not comprised in the monthly instalments of new publications received overland'. The result was that there was no nucleus of books for 'literary and scientific souls' and that residents were left to their 'own researches to acquire a knowledge of the phenomena, statistics, and history of our own immediate locality'.[61]

Debates about the ephemeral versus permanent qualities of collections were therefore related to the types of reading they were seen to encourage: surface/light reading versus that of depth/serious reading. The perception that colonial societies had few 'serious' readers was widespread in the early- to mid-nineteenth century.[62] A short poem by Frederick Brooks in *South African Grins* for 1825 noted that: 'Reading in short is no great passion / Indeed 'tis not at all the fashion'.[63] Brooks's sense that the literary tastes of the colonial reading public were not developed enough to appreciate the best writers is echoed by other commentators. When the English poet R. H. Horne, residing in Melbourne from 1853 to 1869, wrote to the editor of the Melbourne *Age* in 1856 recommending a number of books for purchase by the MPL, he also noted that 'my literary friends in England—philosophers, classicists, novelists, dramatists, and lyric poets, must forgive my silence in respect to them. They need no audience here; neither is the audience they want at present to be found sufficiently numerous to make it worthwhile to venture the introduction'.[64] The *Age* similarly noted in 1856 that 'it must be admitted that the habits of the colonists in general are the reverse of studious; the circumstances of society here tend rather to destroy than foster the taste for intellectual pursuits'.[65]

Notwithstanding its prevalence, this view of Melbourne's literary culture in the mid-nineteenth century was largely misplaced: literacy rates among white settlers both in Melbourne and across the southern hemisphere were relatively high, and the demand for reading material was voracious, with Sydney and Melbourne importing one third of all British book exports in 1854 and nearly half by the 1880s. At the same time, however, there was a growing sense across all the southern colonies that recreational material in public libraries had to be balanced by access to serious reference collections, both to prevent their supposed inundation by loungers and loafers, and to mitigate against the perceived anti-intellectualism of colonial society.[66]

The tensions between fashionable or light literature and serious reading evolved into debates about the value of new, modern texts as opposed to 'dated', standard works. The libraries' approaches to the question of newness versus datedness differ according to their origins, time, and place. Given the SL's status as a subscription library committed to the entertainment of its subscribers, it is unsurprising that it had a policy emphasising the 'newness' of books purchased, requiring any order of 'standard' works of fiction to be 'authorised by the Committee of Management' whereas the purchase of the most recent works of fiction was allowed at the agent's discretion.[67] The SL also framed the access granted to different classes according to the 'newness' of works, with the 1847 library bye-laws stating that Class 4 subscribers could not borrow any book or periodical that had been in the library for less than three months.[68] The SL eventually sourced their material from Mudie's remainders, which meant they had a steady supply of recent fiction and also explains the high percentage of women novelists, noted above, in their collections. The ordering policy stressing novelty is evident in the popularity of contemporary authors (according to numbers of titles held).[69] Unsurprisingly, Walter Scott tops the 1863 catalogue list of imaginative writers with 48 titles, but he is closely followed by G. P. R. James (33 titles), William Hazlitt (21 titles), and Edward Bulwer-Lytton (20 titles).[70]

The ASL employed a similar strategy with its London agent J. M. Richardson. In 1847, directions were sent to Richardson specifying standing orders for the works of Dickens, Bulwer-Lytton, Trollope, Disraeli, Warren, Lever, and Maxwell to be sent as published. As early as 1829, the ASL Committee was attentive to the need for contemporary fiction but with a qualifying condition, specifying in a letter to its colonial agent, Barnard, that he should purchase 'any other recent Novels which may have been reviewed and Approved by the Writers of the Edinburgh or Quarterly Review'.[71] The SALMI's catalogues similarly reveal their commitment to obtaining and advertising their collection of popular novelists. The 1848 catalogue records these best-collected novelists and their latest works under sub-headings of the author's name, such as 'Bulwer's Works', and includes Scott (26 titles); Bulwer-Lytton (12 titles); G. P. R. James (12 titles); and Dickens (11 titles).[72] The novelists with the most titles in the 1851 catalogue include William Harrison Ainsworth (11), Fredrika Bremer (9), Bulwer-Lytton (17), James Fenimore Cooper (34), Daniel Defoe (10), Charles Dickens (11), Benjamin Disraeli (7), Maria Edgeworth (8), Catherine Gore (46), G. P. R. James (46), Charles James Lever (9), Frederick Marryat (23), Walter Scott (26, plus 21 duplicates), William Makepeace Thackeray (8), and Frances Trollope (27).[73]

Many of these novelists are also featured in the SAPL catalogues of the 1840s. The best-represented novelists in the 1842 catalogue include Scott (32 titles), Marryat (19 titles), Edgeworth (17 titles), and G. P. R. James (12 titles).[74] The 1846 catalogue lists works of amusement only by title, except where the authors are well known. The inclusion of names of authors—such as Cooper, Gore, Marryat, and Trollope—alongside their works is suggestive of the popularity of these novelists.[75] The SAPL's interactions with their suppliers further emphasises the importance of their collection staying current. Like the ASL, J. M. Richardson was the supplier for the SAPL, but the committee frequently records their frustration with him for not supplying new books quickly enough. In 1849 the committee notes a decision to appoint a new agent and bookseller because the library is 'not being promptly supplied with the best and newest publications'.[76] Their next appointment as agent, Edward William Brayley, librarian of the London Institution, was similarly dismissed in 1850 because of the delayed arrival of publications. The SAPL's final decision to appoint the publishing and distribution house of Smith, Elder & Co. as their suppliers shows the need for the prompt and steady supply of new purchases. The committee noted that Smith, Elder & Co. has 'constant communications with India' and are therefore 'aware of the departure from London of all vessels bound for the East, by which supplies of books may be continually forwarded'.[77] Smith, Elder & Co. were also, for a time, agents for the SL and the SALMI, suggesting their importance as distributors in Southeast Asia and the southern colonies.

THE SYMBOLIC POWER OF THE COLONIAL LIBRARY CATALOGUE

As well as being guides to the library shelves, it is important not to underestimate the role of the catalogue in establishing the status and title of a public library, and conversely, of unwittingly reflecting the deficiencies and downturns in the fortunes of the institutions. The printed ASL catalogues of the early period of the library's existence, for example, were rudimentary lists, haphazardly arranging works by author or title. After the downturn in the library's financial fortunes in the 1840s, only three partial catalogues would appear in the last twenty years of its existence. A letter to the editor in the *Sydney Morning Herald* in 1869 noted that 'Sydney is destitute of anything deserving the name of a public library. A mass of novels in the one case, and a mass of books without a published catalogue in the other, I should blush to call a public library'. The same contributor pointed out that the catalogue of a public library should itself 'be a creditable affair, both classified and explanatory. The population is worthy of it'.[78] In contrast to the experience of the ASL, the SAPL had eminently scholarly, well-produced catalogues almost from its establishment. As mentioned in Chap. 1, from 1829, Alexander Jardine based his book classification system on that of the French bibliographer J. C. Brunet, whose four-volume *Manuel du Libraire* was in the library's collection and was widely regarded to be of 'decided superiority over every other bibliographic treatise' of the period.[79]

These kinds of prestige catalogues contained symbolic and political power that could be used to form important networks of knowledge exchange, enhance and build collections, and develop new systems for organising knowledge. The MPL catalogues of 1861 and 1865 are prime examples of how prestige catalogues could be used to promote the interests of colonial libraries and foster transnational intellectual and print networks. Designed by Edward La Trobe Bateman (who also designed the library's Queens' Hall Reading Room), with engravings by Samuel Calvert, and printed by Clarson, Shallard & Co., the first official catalogue issued by the MPL Trustees in 1861 was designed to reflect the prestige of the library's collection. Over 700 pages long, it lists 26,723 volumes and contains a detailed preface about the history of the library, its rules and regulations, records of the 'monies voted by Parliament', a sample bequest form for patrons, and the layout of the library building.[80] That the catalogue was viewed as a promotional opportunity for both the library and the colony of Victoria is clear from the £500 allocated towards its creation, and the effort put into its design, which features botanical illustrations, in particular, 'decorated Initials and Finals' by Bateman that reflected the 'flora of the country', and are the first example of 'Australian flora being used for decorative motifs'.[81] As Brian Hubber has noted, 'presentation copies were often large paper copies, printed in a combination of red and black, and specially bound in green or red morocco leather inscribed in gilt', and used to raise the profile of the library.[82]

The 1861 catalogue was celebrated by the local press, being described as 'handsomely printed, characteristically ornamented, and sold at the very moderate price of half-a-crown', thereby supporting a wide circulation. 'Compiled with unwearying diligence and with singular accuracy', its form was also praised for its utility and for encouraging a wide range of users, including students who would 'doubtless find possession' of the catalogue 'of much service as with it they can find out without going to the library what books are available in it on any given subject'.[83] As this observation suggests, the catalogue could itself support a culture of self-help, as it could direct access to library material on the shelves without library mediation. Panizzi's rejection of specialist classifications in the 1849 BML catalogue, for example, was part of his object of making scholarship accessible to all.[84] The MPL's adoption of Panizzi's alphabetical catalogue, with the addition of a classificatory index, was done for similar reasons. Catalogues were thus an important expression of the role of a public library in making 'information accessible to all' and 'knowledge transparent'.[85]

Praising the structure of the MPL catalogue, the Melbourne *Herald* noted that the 'alphabetical list of authors' was the cataloguing system 'adopted at all the great libraries in England, from the British Museum and the Bodleian downwards'.[86] The SAI was particularly impressed by the classificatory system used by the MPL. The Governor of South Australia used his 1879 address to point out the efficacy of the MPL's arrangement, which 'affords facility to the student to acquire substantial information from works bearing on his enquiries, and without interruptions which are likely to arise in the absence of such classification'.[87] As early as 1863, the *South Australian Weekly Chronicle* was arguing in response to the 'defective' SAI catalogue that 'a perfect catalogue must be a double one; first of all books arranged under the names of the authors, and secondly a list of all books classified with reference to the subjects upon which they treat'.[88] Although not explicitly named, this arrangement was the one used by the MPL.

The Melbourne *Herald* recognised that the 1861 MPL catalogue had a 'political' value in addition to its 'biographical' and 'literary' value, arguing that the catalogue provides evidence of the 'public spirit, the intelligence and the high civilisation of this community. To any foreigner of large scientific or literary attainments, here is ample proof that the colonists of Victoria are something more and better than a keenly money-seeking set of people'. 'All this', declared the *Herald*, a man 'in London, or Paris, or Rome, may learn from the new catalogue'.[89] Even Queen Victoria is reported as 'particularly admir[ing] the printing and general embellishments of the book, so creditable to the taste and skill of the designers and artisans of Melbourne'.[90] The catalogue was, moreover, used as a way of securing donations from other institutions and intellectual societies. During his visit to London in 1865, the MPL librarian, Augustus Tulk, presented the MPL catalogue to the Department of India and to the Society of Antiquaries as a means of celebrating their relationships and securing donations. The Melbourne *Leader* reported that Tulk had secured a donation of 400 volumes (Society of Antiquaries) with a further 500–600 volumes expected (Department of India). A letter from the secretary of the Society of Antiquaries gives us a sense of how the catalogue was received: 'I need scarcely assure the trustees that the greatest admiration was expressed at the very sumptuous and artistic embellishments which adorn this really princely work'.[91]

Records of donations in the 1860s demonstrate the international prestige of the MPL even beyond the Anglophone world, with a list of benefactors including the British government; the Prussian government; the British Museum; the government of the Netherlands; the Emperor of France, Napoleon III; and Victor Emmanuel, King of Italy.[92] The Trustees' Report of 1870–1871 shows how important the cultivation of these relationships could be, as donated works made up almost a fifth of the MPL's collection.[93] Although an extensive collection of donations were presented by foreign governments and consuls, the MPL ensured it also cultivated intercolonial relationships, receiving a number of donations from its colonial neighbours including Tasmania, Queensland, and New Zealand. Government officials and eminent Victorian citizens were not remiss in their philanthropic duties, with figures such as Governors La Trobe and Barkly, the engineer Major-General Charles Pasley, and the scientist Georg von Neumayer giving generously.[94] The ASL did not benefit from the same level of attention from public benefactors, but its members did donate books, including their own writings, such as Thomas Mitchell's donation of his *Three Expeditions to the Interior of Eastern Australia* (1838). As Heather Gaunt has noted, the TPL actively sought to acquire international publications, and its 1872 *Annual Report* noted 'a munificent gift of Books, Maps, Plans, and Charts from her Majesty's Government', as well as gifts from the governments of Tasmania, Fiji, New Zealand, and the United States, and from learned societies in England, Ireland, and Mauritius. 'Such recognitions' were considered 'the best proofs which can be adduced of the status which the Library has attained'.[95]

Sizable donations and bequests, such as the Dessin and Grey donations to the SAPL, and the Bicheno bequest to the TPL, could significantly shape the character and future of a public library's collection and purpose. William Tyrrell-Glynn describes the Dessinian Collection as an 'infectious example' in 'promoting the concept of a library especially created for the use of the general public free of charge', which 'probably gave rise to the idea' of the SAPL.[96] A substantial gift from George Grey in the 1860s significantly augmented the prestige of the SAPL. Grey's donation—itself partly 'the united collection of two very eminent wealthy bibliomaniacs'— included 114 medieval and Renaissance manuscripts (many in contemporary bindings), a large number of early printed works and other rare items, and a vast collection of the earliest examples of printing in hitherto oral languages from Africa, Asia, and the Pacific.[97] Prestige catalogues provided a means of curating these collections. In 1852, elated by the significant acquisition of the Bicheno bequest, the TPL produced a catalogue which divided its entire collection into the 'Bicheno collection' and a 'Tasmanian Public Library' collection.[98]

Whether the catalogues and collections of these emerging public libraries met the rapidly changing needs of their colonies was always a contentious issue, but they do indicate an awareness of the specificity of their responsibilities to the distinctive social, cultural, and political conditions of the southern colonies. The collections, catalogues, and reports discussed in this chapter demonstrate the libraries' efforts to transform 'a mob of light readers'—accused of treating books as women treated bonnets—into a community of politically educated and respectable colonists who could, in some instances, eventually achieve and maintain responsible government.[99] Catalogues, as the next chapter will show, could also provide new forms of taxonomic knowledge, playing a crucial role in the development of a 'taxonomic state' motivated by the belief that knowing and understanding the 'native mind' could inform 'native policy'.[100]

Notes

1. *Proceedings*, SAPL, 1848, 13: http://www.ucd.ie/southhem/record.html#464.
2. *Catalogue*, SAPL, 1842, iii: http://www.ucd.ie/southhem/record.html#269.
3. *Proceedings*, SAPL, 1849, 19, 18: http://www.ucd.ie/southhem/record.html#465.
4. *Report of the Trustees of the Public Library, Museums, and National Gallery of Victoria, with the Reports of the Sectional Committees, for the Year 1870–71* (Melbourne: John Ferres, Government Printer, 1871), 12, accessed August 9, 2018: https://www.parliament.vic.gov.au/vufind/Record/90063.
5. Lewis C. Roberts, 'Disciplining and Disinfecting Working-Class Readers in the Victorian Public Library', *Victorian Literature and Culture* 26, no. 1 (1998): 105–132 (108, 113).
6. *Sydney Morning Herald*, February 23, 1844, 2.
7. *Proceedings*, SAPL, 1849, 7: http://www.ucd.ie/southhem/record.html#465.
8. *Proceedings at the 12th Anniversary Meeting of Subscribers to the Public Library, Cape Town, Cape of Good Hope, Thursday, 29 April 1841* (Cape Town: s. n., 1841), 5.
9. James Hole, *An Essay of the History and Management of Literary, Scientific, & Mechanics' Institutions* (London: Longman, 1853), 27–28.
10. Martin Lyons, 'New Readers in the Nineteenth Century: Women, Children, Workers', in *A History of Reading in the West*, ed. Guglielmo Cavallo and Roger Chartier, trans. Lydia G. Cochrane (Amherst: University of Michigan, 1997), 313–344 (335).
11. Christine Pawley, 'Beyond Market Models and Resistance: Organizations as a Middle Layer in the History of Reading', *The Library Quarterly: Information, Community, Policy* 79, no. 1 (January 2009): 73–93 (84–5).
12. *Proceedings*, SAPL, 1857, 13, 12, 16–18, 24: http://www.ucd.ie/southhem/record.html#471.
13. *Proceedings*, SAPL, 1857, 24: http://www.ucd.ie/southhem/record.html#471.

14. *Singapore Free Press and Mercantile Advertiser*, August 24, 1843, 2.
15. Brendan Luyt, 'The Importance of Fiction to the Raffles Library, Singapore, During the Long Nineteenth-Century', *Library & Information History* 25, no. 2 (2009): 117–131 (123).
16. *South Australian Register* (Adelaide), February 3, 1857, 2.
17. *Tasmanian Times* (Hobart), January 29, 1868, 2.
18. *Age* (Melbourne), February 20, 1856, 3.
19. *Catalogue*, SAPL, 1826: http://www.ucd.ie/southhem/record.html#449.
20. *Proceedings*, SAPL, 1849, 30: http://www.ucd.ie/southhem/record.html#465.
21. 'Report of the Committee of the Raffles Library and Museum, for the year ending December 31st 1874', in *Straits Settlements, Annual Reports for the Year 1874* (Singapore: Government Printing Office, 1875), 121.
22. Possibly Julius Vogel, then Premier of New Zealand and later the author of the utopian novel *Anno Domini 2000, or, Woman's Destiny* (1889).
23. *Straits Observer* (Singapore), December 28, 1874, 2.
24. *South Australian Register*, July 1, 1850, 3.
25. *South Australian Register*, June 26, 1850, 4.
26. *South Australian Register*, September 14, 1847, 2.
27. Priya Joshi, *In Another County: Colonialism, Culture and the English Novel in India* (New York: Columbia University Press, 2002), 62.
28. *Catalogue*, FPL, 1869: www.ucd.ie/southhem/record.html#502.
29. *Protestant Standard* (Sydney), October 9, 1869, 3.
30. See, for example, *Catalogue of the Free Public Library, Sydney* (Sydney: Government Printer, 1872). For the holdings of the FPL's reference and lending libraries, see *Sydney Morning Herald*, May 22, 1878, 3.
31. Heather Gaunt, 'Identity and Nation in the Australian Public Library: The Development of Local and National Collections 1850s–1940s, Using the Tasmanian Public Library as Case Study' (PhD diss., University of Tasmania, 2010), 53, accessed August 6, 2018: https://eprints.utas.edu.au/10772/2/Gaunt_whole.pdf.
32. Bicheno stipulated in his will that the books be offered to the TPL for a reduced sum. *Catalogue*, TPL, 1852, iv: http://www.ucd.ie/southhem/record.html#327.
33. *Catalogue*, MPL, 1861, v: http://www.ucd.ie/southhem/record.html#112.
34. *Report of the Trustees of the Public Library*, 1871, 15.
35. *Catalogue*, MPL, 1861, v: http://www.ucd.ie/southhem/record.html#112.
36. Redmond Barry letter to Edward Barnard, quoted in Richard Overell, 'The Melbourne Public Library and the Guillaumes: The Relationship between a Colonial Library and its London Book Supplier 1854–1865', in *Peopling a Profession: Papers from the Fourth Forum on Australian Library History, Monash University, 25 and 26 September 1989*, ed. Frank Upward and Jean P. Whyte (Melbourne: Ancora Press, 1991), 35.

37. *Report of the Trustees of the Public Library*, 1871, 17–19.
38. *Catalogue*, MPL, 1861: http://www.ucd.ie/southhem/record.html#112.
39. *Catalogue*, MPL, 1854: http://www.ucd.ie/southhem/record.html#81.
40. Porscha Fermanis, 'British Cultures of Reading and Literary Appreciation in Nineteenth-Century Singapore', in *The Edinburgh History of Reading: A World Survey from Antiquity to Present*, ed. Mary Hammond and Jonathan Rose (Edinburgh: Edinburgh University Press), forthcoming 2019, n.p.
41. *Catalogue*, SL, 1863, http://www.ucd.ie/southhem/record.html#131; *Catalogue*, MPL, 1861, http://www.ucd.ie/southhem/record.html#112.
42. *Catalogue*, MPL, c.1867: http://www.ucd.ie/southhem/record.html#163.
43. *Catalogue*, MPL, 1861: http://handle.slv.vic.gov.au/10381/243167.
44. *Catalogue*, MPL, 1861: http://www.ucd.ie/southhem/record.html#112.
45. Brian Hubber, 'Leading by Example: Barry in the Library', *La Trobe Journal* 73 (Autumn 2004): 67–74 (73).
46. *Herald* (Melbourne), March 28, 1862, 4; *Report of the Trustees of the Public Library*, 1871, 23.
47. Michael Talbot, 'A Close Affiliation: Coordination of Institutes in South Australia', in *Pioneering Culture: Mechanics' Institutes and Schools of Arts in Australia*, ed. Philip C. Candy and John Laurent (Adelaide: Auslib Press, 1994), 335–356 (341).
48. *South Australian Register*, January 30, 1861, 3.
49. *South Australian Register*, October 14, 1858, 3.
50. *South Australian Weekly Chronicle* (Adelaide), October 31, 1863, 4.
51. *Catalogue*, SAPL, 1842, 162: http://www.ucd.ie/southhem/record.html#269.
52. *Proceedings*, SAPL, 1857, 12: http://www.ucd.ie/southhem/record.html#471.
53. Luyt, 'The Importance of Fiction to the Raffles Library', 119.
54. On annotated catalogues, see Paul Sturges and Alison Barr, '"The fiction nuisance" in Nineteenth-Century British Public Libraries', *Journal of Librarianship and Information Science* 24, no. 1 (1991): 23–31 (25).
55. *South Australian Register*, January 30, 1861, 3.
56. *Proceedings*, SAPL, 1857, 23: http://www.ucd.ie/southhem/record.html#471.
57. *Report of the Trustees of the Public Library*, 1871, 14.
58. *South Australian Register*, January 30, 1861, 3.
59. *Report of the Trustees of the Public Library*, 1871, 12.
60. *Argus* (Melbourne), May 9, 1887, 7, quoted in Gaunt, 'Identity and Nation in the Australian Public Library', 286.
61. *Straits Times* (Singapore), September 30, 1846, 3.

62. See, for example, Wallace Kirsop, 'Libraries for an Imperial Power', in *The Cambridge History of Libraries in Britain and Ireland Volume II 1640–1850*, ed. Giles Mandelbrote and K. A. Manley (Cambridge: Cambridge University Press, 2006), 494–508.
63. Quoted in P. R. Coates, 'National Library of South Africa', in *The International Dictionary of Library Histories: Volume 1 & 2*, ed. David H. Stam (New York: Routledge, 2001), 573–575 (574).
64. *Age* (Melbourne), July 28, 1856, 5.
65. *Age*, February 18, 1856, 3.
66. Malcolm Wood, *Australia's Secular Foundations* (Melbourne: Australian Scholarly Publishing, 2016), 66. *Free Press and Mercantile Advertiser*, August 24, 1843, 2.
67. *The Second Report of the Singapore Library, 1846* (Singapore: G. M. Frederick at the Singapore Free Press Office, 1846), 12.
68. *The Third Report of the Singapore Library, 1847* (Singapore: G. M. Frederick at the Singapore Free Press Office, 1847), 4.
69. *The 15th Report of the Singapore Library* (Singapore: Free Press Office, 1860), 3.
70. *Catalogue*, SL, 1863: http://www.ucd.ie/southhem/record.html#131.
71. ASL, *Minutes and Proceedings, 1826–1846*, October 12, 1829, *Australian Library and Literary Institution Papers, 1826–1871*, Manuscript, State Library of New South Wales, A1625.
72. *Catalogue*, SALMI, 1848: http://www.ucd.ie/southhem/record.html#49.
73. *Catalogue*, SALMI, 1851: http://www.ucd.ie/southhem/record.html#77.
74. *Catalogue*, SAPL, 1842: http://www.ucd.ie/southhem/record.html#269.
75. *Catalogue*, SAPL, 1846: http://www.ucd.ie/southhem/record.html#462.
76. *Proceedings*, SAPL, 1849, 2: http://www.ucd.ie/southhem/record.html#465.
77. *Proceedings*, SAPL, 1850, 5: http://www.ucd.ie/southhem/record.html#466.
78. *Sydney Morning Herald*, March 5, 1869, 3.
79. 'Libraries', *North American Review* 45, no. 96 (1837): 116–148 (148). *Catalogue*, SAPL, 1829: http://www.ucd.ie/southhem/record.html#264.
80. *Catalogue*, MPL, 1861: http://www.ucd.ie/southhem/record.html#112.
81. Daniel Thomas, 'Bateman, Edward La Trobe (1815–1897)', *Australian Dictionary of Biography*, accessed August 2, 2018: http://adb.anu.edu.au/biography/bateman-edward-la-trobe-2951/text4285.
82. Hubber, 'Leading by Example: Barry in the Library', 70.
83. *Argus*, March 28, 1862, 4.
84. Marvin Spevack, 'The Impact of the British Museum Library', in *The Cambridge History of Libraries in Britain and Ireland Volume II 1640–1850*, ed. Giles Mandelbrote and K. A. Manley (Cambridge: Cambridge University Press, 2006), 422–437 (435).

85. Patrick Joyce, 'The Politics of the Liberal Archive', *History of the Human Sciences* 12, no. 3 (1999): 35–49 (41).
86. *Herald*, March 28, 1862, 4–5.
87. *The South Australian Institute: Comprising the Public Library, Art Gallery, and Museums* (Adelaide: W. K. Thomas & Co, 1879), 15, accessed August 4, 2018: http://www.slsa.sa.gov.au/archivaldocs/d/South_Australian_Institute_addresses_1879.pdf.
88. *South Australian Weekly Chronicle* (Adelaide), October 31, 1863, 4.
89. *Herald*, March 28, 1862, 4.
90. *Leader* (Melbourne), October 17, 1863, 8.
91. *Leader*, May 6, 1865, 2.
92. *Catalogue*, MPL, 1861: http://www.ucd.ie/southhem/record.html#112; *Catalogue*, MPL, 1865: http://www.ucd.ie/southhem/record.html#147; *Catalogue*, MPL, 1867: http://www.ucd.ie/southhem/record.html#163.
93. *Report of the Trustees of the Public Library*, 1871, 12.
94. *Catalogue*, MPL, 1861: http://www.ucd.ie/southhem/record.html#112; *Catalogue*, MPL, 1865: http://www.ucd.ie/southhem/record.html#147; *Catalogue*, MPL, 1867: http://www.ucd.ie/southhem/record.html#163.
95. Heather Gaunt, '"In the Pursuit of Colonial Intelligence", The Archive and Identity in the Australian Colonies in the Nineteenth Century', in *Information Beyond Borders: International Cultural and Intellectual Exchange in the Belle Époque*, ed. W. Boyd Rayward (London and New York: Routledge, 2016), 49–68 (53).
96. W. H. P. A. Tyrrell-Glynn, 'The History of the South African Public Library, 1830–1961' (PhD diss., University of Stellenbosch, 1983), 90.
97. *Argus*, March 24, 1862, 6.
98. *Catalogue*, TPL, 1852: http://www.ucd.ie/southhem/record.html#327.
99. *Age*, February 18, 1856, 3.
100. Ann L. Stoler, *Carnal Knowledge and Imperial Power: Race and the Invention of Colonial Rule* (Berkeley: University of California Press, 2002), 206.

Open Access This chapter is licensed under the terms of the Creative Commons Attribution 4.0 International License (http://creativecommons.org/licenses/by/4.0/), which permits use, sharing, adaptation, distribution and reproduction in any medium or format, as long as you give appropriate credit to the original author(s) and the source, provide a link to the Creative Commons licence and indicate if changes were made.

The images or other third party material in this chapter are included in the chapter's Creative Commons licence, unless indicated otherwise in a credit line to the material. If material is not included in the chapter's Creative Commons licence and your intended use is not permitted by statutory regulation or exceeds the permitted use, you will need to obtain permission directly from the copyright holder.

CHAPTER 5

Knowing the 'Native Mind': Ethnological and Philological Collections

Abstract This chapter examines the role that the major research libraries of the southern colonies played in the collection, classification, and transmission of ethnological and philological knowledge about Indigenous populations. It argues that the transnational scientific networks, useful knowledge societies, and periodicals cultivated by public libraries enabled colonial cities such as Melbourne, Singapore, and Cape Town to become regional centres of scientific knowledge creation as well as collection, influencing both British governmental policy and broader cultural attitudes amongst Europeans towards the Indigenous peoples of the expanding British Empire.

Keywords Ethnology • Philology • George Grey • Wilhelm Bleek • James Richardson Logan

As Richard Macmahon has recently argued, racial classification was central to the 'political narratives' that governed international relations, the politics of social class, and modern ideas about social and cultural development between 1840 and the Second World War.[1] In this reading, racial classification emerges as a 'transdisciplinary' project aimed at associating 'biological racial types with cultural nations' through 'assemblages of physical, psychological and cultural traits'.[2] These assemblages provided the empirical ballast to support racialist ideologies that argued for the innate superiority of European peoples and were used to justify the subjugation of Indigenous peoples in the colonies—ideologies that proved remarkably resilient through nearly one hundred years of profound political and social change.

Book holdings were critical to the way in which this knowledge about the peoples of the colonies was ordered, and therefore played an important role in the development of racial thinking. The collections of influential colonial intellectuals and administrators such as George Grey have already been analysed by historians for the symbolic 'cultural capital' they endowed upon the public libraries to which they donated. Saul Dubow has argued that Grey's 1861 gift of philological, ethnological, folklore, and antiquarian works to the SAPL 'signified that the Cape was not only an outlying outpost of the British Empire but also a European bridgehead into Africa'.[3] While the collection of reference works on regional topics was undoubtedly part of an effort to raise the status of these institutions both nationally and across the Anglo-world, as Dubow suggests, the collection of ethnological and philological 'data' on Indigenous peoples was also imbricated with the political mission of moral colonisation. As Alan Lester has persuasively argued, Grey's collections and writings about Australia, New Zealand, and South Africa formed 'an extraordinarily potent and geographically extensive ethnographic-governmental assemblage' that served to justify a colonial policy increasingly aimed at enacting cultural genocide against the Indigenous inhabitants of Australia, South Africa, and New Zealand in the name of moral colonisation and 'enlightened' social progress.[4]

Developing Colonial Ethnological and Anthropological Collections c. 1840–1870

The development of scientific reference collections in colonial public libraries was uneven and piecemeal. We argued in Chap. 4 that the financial need to cater to the demands of the general reader meant that even those libraries that aspired to establish themselves as research libraries, such as the SAPL, were constrained by the necessity to tailor their acquisitions towards the preference of subscribers for light and general reading. 'Science' made up only between 0% and 14% of the libraries' holdings between 1829 and 1862. In the 1860s, the SAPL and the MPL held the largest 'Science' holdings at 12% and 14%, respectively (see Appendix C, Tables C.3 and C.6). The encounter narratives of scientific and gentleman travellers, and contemporary emigration guides, on the other hand, were particularly well stocked in libraries across the southern colonies throughout the period 1825 to 1869. Looking across the collections of the SAPL, SAI, and SL, we can see that encounter narratives, travelogues, and emigration guides, all of which were habitually categorised under the rubric 'Geography, Voyages, and Travels', made up between 11% and 28% of these libraries' total book holdings during this period (see Appendix C).[5]

As well as being very popular with general readers, and providing settlers with a means of gathering information about the environment they lived in, the personal observations of travellers and missionaries recorded in encounter narratives are widely acknowledged to have played a central role in the development of the ethnological theories of nineteenth-century practitioners of the 'sciences of man'.[6] The incorporation of historiography, political science, and antiquarian inquiry alongside comparative philology and comparative anatomy as the main fields of scholarly inquiry pursued by ethnologists illustrates the 'transdisciplinarity' of what Macmahon has termed the 'philosophical ethnology' that dominated British scholarship between 1840 and 1860.[7] Yet for all that this 'philosophical ethnology' was an incorporative discipline, integrating the scientific, linguistic, historical, and political insights found in ethnographic encounter narratives and government reports, there were some important differences between ethnological writings and the more anecdotal encounter narratives categorised in colonial libraries under 'voyages and travels'. Most fundamentally, practitioners of ethnology in the nineteenth century produced formal taxonomies of human cultures informed by the Linnean classificatory procedures that had shaped the formation of natural history as a discipline in the eighteenth century.[8]

While there is considerable variation in the ways in which individual librarians ordered the knowledge accumulated by these institutions, it is evident that 'voyages and travels' was always classified as a distinct literary genre that was more frequently aligned with history than with natural history.[9] In the 1877 catalogue of the RLM in Singapore, for example, 'travels, voyages, adventures and explorations, including general descriptions of countries, which embrace a personal narrative', are one category, stressing the personal, anecdotal, and subjective quality of these ethnographic encounter narratives. This category is distinct from 'natural history and ethnology',[10] which are amalgamated into one category to reflect the disciplinary history of ethnology as a sub-discipline of natural history—one that formally emerged as a science in its own right in the late 1840s and 1850s.[11] The disciplinary interrelationship between natural history and ethnology is also reflected in the subject classes adapted by Fredrick Maskew, the SAPL's second librarian. The 1862 SAPL catalogue classifies 'ethnology' as a sub-discipline within the broader rubric of 'natural history', which also includes botany, zoology, mineralogy, and geology, as well as the more practical natural sciences of agriculture and gardening.[12]

The status of ethnology as a protean discipline yet to emerge fully from its disciplinary entanglement with comparative philology in the 1840s and 1850s is reflected in the absence of ethnology as a distinct category of scientific inquiry in the extant library catalogues prior to 1858. In the catalogues of the SAPL, the first library in the southern colonies to acquire an extensive scientific and reference collection, works of comparative anatomy are classified under 'Surgery and medicine',[13] while the only work to explicitly engage with the anatomical classification of human beings, Scottish lawyer and phrenologist George Combe's *System of Phrenology* (1825), is classified under chemistry.[14] The first library in the southern colonies to list ethnological works in its scientific reference collections was the MPL. The 1858 catalogue supplied by the MPL's London bookseller J. J. Guillaume includes works by leading British ethnologists James Cowles Prichard and Robert Knox.[15] Prichard and Robert Gordan Latham, whose work is listed in the MPL catalogue for 1859, are the two figures credited by historians of nineteenth-century science with establishing the disciplinary contours of ethnology.[16] Knox meanwhile dismissed Prichard and Latham's emphasis on the importance of comparative philology to ethnology, instead privileging anatomy as the primary means of comparing and classifying human races.

Sadiah Qureshi has suggested that, although Knox's polygenetic transcendental materialism has often been identified in histories of the development of ethnology and anthropology as a key turning point in what is seen as a mid-century transition to more biologically deterministic views on racial variety, in reality Knox's theories, along with those of fellow polygenesist James Hunt,[17] were 'highly controversial and deemed utterly unacceptable by many of their contemporaries'.[18] An analysis of the ethnology holdings of the public libraries of the colonial southern hemisphere supports Qureshi's assertion that it was Latham's and Prichard's transdisciplinary approach to the study of human variety that was more influential than the biologically deterministic methodology pursued by Knox and Hunt. By the 1860s, the three public libraries in the colonial southern hemisphere that had substantial scientific reference collections that included ethnological works—the MPL, the SAPL, and the SAI—all stocked the major ethnological works of Latham and Prichard but not of Knox or Hunt.[19]

That the works of the two most influential British ethnologists should first appear in the southern colonies in a library whose librarian, Augustus

Tulk, was extremely active in promoting the MPL in Britain and across Europe (see Chap. 4), argues for the importance of strong metropolitan connections in establishing and maintaining up-to-date scientific reference collections in the colonies. Given the MPL's significant annual grant from the Victorian parliament,[20] it is perhaps unsurprising that the MPL's extant catalogues suggest that not only did it have the largest scientific reference collection of any library in the southern colonies, including impressive holdings of scientific periodicals, but that it also kept abreast with the latest developments in the evolving disciplines of ethnology, philology, and anthropology throughout the 1860s. As Wallace Kirsop has noted, Redmond Barry was a 'zealous promoter' of links between the MPL and European scientific bodies, receiving subscriptions to leading German scientific periodicals through the local bookseller Samuel Mullen.[21] Barry was also well-read in comparative philology and attempted in 1866 to undertake research on Aboriginal languages, as well as to develop his so-called Ethnotypical Museum. Although the project did not come to fruition, its aim was to elucidate 'the general laws of Philology which may govern many, if not all, the languages and dialects spoken in Australia'.[22]

The 1860s was an important decade in the development of the sciences of man in Britain. It was also the decade of the formal disciplinary rupture between the monogenesist Ethnological Society of London and James Hunt's more biologically determinist, polygenesist Anthropological Society. The 1861 catalogue for the MPL begins to reflect this disciplinary fragmentation in the sciences of man by maintaining separate subject categories for ethnology, philology, and phrenology.[23] The philology category is particularly extensive with over 140 titles and the catalogue contains a further 70 titles of 'grammars'. The MPL's philology category features works by James Richardson Logan and George Grey (including the catalogue of his philological library collection compiled by Wilhelm Bleek), whose influence on ethnological and philological knowledge will be discussed in more detail below. The 1865 supplementary catalogue to the MPL further adds 'anthropology' as a distinct disciplinary category for the first time, reflecting the disciplinary rupture between ethnologists and anthropologists that had taken place in Britain in 1863 when James Hunt founded the Anthropological Society.[24]

The rise of anthropology as a discipline in the 1860s—one which privileged the physiological and anatomical markers of racial difference over the cultural, linguistic, and historical factors that had been central to ethnological inquiry throughout the 1840s and 1850s—is also reflected in the subject classifications adopted by the SAI in its 1869 catalogue. Here, ethnology is separated from natural history and amalgamated with the medical and anatomical sciences under the category 'Anatomy, Medicine, Physiology, Ethnology etc.'.[25] That metropolitan disciplinary developments, such as the increasing dominance of comparative anatomy in ethnological and anthropological inquiry post-1863, were reflected in the classificatory procedures of public libraries in Victoria and South Australia by 1865 and 1869, respectively, is evidence of the speed with which colonial libraries could respond to metropolitan scientific advances, and their commitment to maintaining scientific reference collections that reflected the latest disciplinary developments in British science.

Regional 'Centres of Collection': Ethnological and Philological Knowledge Collection

While it can be argued that ethnological and philological reference collections in the southern colonies responded to the disciplinary developments in British ethnology, it is equally evident that metropolitan ethnologists and philologists were dependent on data gathered by informants and field collectors in the colonies. The rise of ethnology as a disciplinary field between 1830 and 1860 was facilitated by the expansion of the British Empire in the first half of the nineteenth century, an expansion which 'produced a global network for gathering and exchanging information' as British and Irish professionals of all social classes not only travelled but increasingly sojourned or settled for extended periods in Britain's settler colonies.[26] Between 1820 and 1870 ethnological and philological data collected by actors as varied as missionaries, colonial administrators, members of the armed forces, and professional men of science profoundly shaped the theories about human variety that were developed by the most prominent European ethnologists. In order to illustrate this point further, this section of the chapter will look specifically at the networks of knowledge production and dissemination that gathered around Andrew Smith and the SAPL in Cape Town during the 1820s and 1830s, and James Richardson Logan and the SL in Singapore in the 1840s and 1850s.

Dr Andrew Smith was appointed as the first Superintendent of the South African Museum (SAM) in 1825, an appointment that afforded him the opportunity to gain first-hand experience in the collection and classification of natural historical specimens.[27] This experience, combined with his professional training as a medical doctor, influenced the observational and classificatory practices that he was to bring to his published studies of southern African ethnology and zoology.[28] Shortly after being appointed as Superintendent of the SAM, Smith was appointed to the committee of the SAPL. The SAPL was conceived as an athenaeum, and the acquisition of a serious scientific reference collection for the library coincided with Smith's appointment to its committee. During Smith's year on the SAPL committee, 146 new scientific reference works were purchased by the library, 56 of which pertained to the plant or animal sciences.[29] These included multi-volume English-language editions of major research works in the plant and animal sciences such as the French zoologist Georges-Louis Leclerc, Comte de Buffon's *Natural History* (1749) and the Swedish natural historian Carl Linnaeus's *System of Nature* (1735), both foundational texts for the scholarly study of zoology. The 'medicine' section contained an octavo edition of the prominent British physician William Lawrence's *Lectures on Physiology, Zoology, and the Natural History of Man* (1823), which caused controversy in Britain by using comparative anatomy to promote a materialism that seemed to some contemporary commentators to verge on atheism.[30] The presence of such a controversial and innovative new work of comparative physiology in the SAPL is a testament to Smith and the library committee's commitment to keeping abreast with the latest British developments in the animal and human sciences—a commitment also evidenced by the fact that the library subscribed to the *Transactions of the Royal Society* at this time.[31]

Although Smith only served on the library committee for one year, the SAPL continued to expand its scientific reference collection significantly throughout the 1820s. Works for the library's reference collection were chosen in London by Sir John Barrow, and the public subsidy provided to the library between 1822 and 1829 by a tax on the Cape's lucrative wine trade made the 1820s a uniquely productive period in the library's history for the acquisition of scientific works and learned journals. Of the 1584 titles listed in the 1829 catalogue 289 were scientific, accounting for approximately 21% of the library's book holdings compared to just 6% in 1825 (see Appendix C, Table C.3).[32] As well as reference works, the SAPL also greatly expanded its scientific periodical holdings, subscribing to 11 English, Scottish, and North American scientific periodicals by 1829.[33] A notable acquisition to the 'medicine' section in 1829 was Prichard's *Researches into the Physical History of Mankind* (2nd edn, 1826), arguably the earliest British ethnological work that built upon German naturalist Johann Friedrich Blumenbach's division of mankind into five distinct races, while maintaining the religiously orthodox monogenesist position on the essential unity of mankind.

As well as providing a world-class scientific reference collection, the SAPL's reading rooms in the Cape Town commercial exchange 'functioned as a key intellectual and cultural brokerage centre, as well as serving as a clublike meeting place for the exchange of news and views'.[34] Dubow has argued that the SAPL played a key role in facilitating the forms of gentlemanly sociability that were central to the development of networks of scientific knowledge production and exchange in the era before the widespread professionalisation of the sciences in the late-nineteenth century. Central to this function was the use of the SAPL's meeting rooms by the SI (1829–1831), the Cape Colony's first learned society devoted to the study of science. Modelled on the literary and philosophical societies that were forming in the recently industrialised towns of Britain, the SI shared with these metropolitan societies a focus on the production of local knowledge. Like the Australian philosophical societies formed in a similar period, the SI aimed not simply to debate metropolitan scientific advances and developments, but also to contribute to bodies of knowledge about its immediate locality.[35]

To achieve this, the SI encouraged British and Dutch settlers based in southern Africa to read papers at its monthly meetings. The majority of the papers read at the monthly meetings were published in the SI's journal, the *South African Quarterly Journal* (*SAQJ*), Africa's first scientific journal. The purpose of the *SAQJ* was to disseminate to an international audience local knowledge relating to the economic and natural productions of southern Africa.[36] Papers read at the SI between 1829 and 1831 and published in the *SAQJ* included lectures on the horticulture of the Western Cape; lectures on the history of the Cape of Good Hope; and Andrew Smith's zoological researches on the wildlife of southern Africa and ethnological papers on the Indigenous southern African San or 'bushman' people.[37]

While Smith's contribution to South African zoology is widely acknowledged, what is less well recognised is his influence on British ethnology.[38] Although he never published his planned monograph on South African ethnology, Smith's ethnological notes on the San 'bushmen' were circulated to a transnational audience of colonial and metropolitan ethnologists through the pages of the *SAQJ*, enabling ethnological data gathered in the furthest reaches of the colonial periphery to influence the thinking of those at the very heart of British ethnology. In his 1848 address to the Ethnological Society of London, Prichard described the *SAQJ* as 'an excellent journal of scientific and historical information'.[39] Smith's 'Notes and observations on the bushmen' profoundly influenced Prichard's own writings on southern African Indigenous peoples in his *Natural History of Man* (1844), a work that has been identified by historians of ethnology and anthropology as key in the establishment and popularisation of ethnology in Britain.[40]

The emergence of the SAPL in the 1820s as both a repository for the collection of the latest scientific reference works, and as a venue where useful knowledge societies such as the SI could meet, and scientific knowledge could be debated and disseminated, created the institutional conditions necessary for the flourishing of the ethnological and zoological sciences in the Cape Colony during the 1820s and 1830s. The support of prominent men of science such as Smith and Sir John Herschel for the Cape Colony's early useful knowledge societies, and their use of the *SAQJ* as a means of disseminating research done in the Cape to an international audience, enabled local knowledge gathered in the furthest reaches of the southern African interior to reach the heart of the metropolitan scientific establishment.

The SL meanwhile reflected Singapore's location within the broader network of British East India by stocking a large number of periodicals and newspapers from India, as well as specifically targeting 'any valuable new publications on India, China, or other Eastern British Settlement' which were 'to have the first consideration on all occasions'.[41] This move towards collecting more locally focused and specialised ethnographic materials reflected the library's growing aspiration throughout the period 1840–1870 to establish itself as a serious reference library. As early as the 1840s, there were calls in the Anglophone press for the emergence of a literary and scientific association in Singapore in order to provide a forum for the production and dissemination of scientific knowledge about Singapore and the Straits Settlements.[42] These calls were answered by James Richardson Logan, owner of the *Pinang Gazette* (est. 1838) and founder of the *Journal of the Indian Archipelago and Eastern Asia* (*JIA*) (est. 1847). Logan was the first colonial intellectual in Singapore to make a conscious effort to try to establish Singapore as a centre for the production of knowledge about East Asia and the Malay Peninsula. This aspiration was enabled through Logan's connections to both intra-imperial and trans-regional networks of scientific knowledge exchange. He was a fellow of the Royal Geographic Society, a member of the Asiatic Society of Bengal, and a corresponding member of the Ethnological Society of London and the Batavian Society of Arts and Sciences. As well as contributing to the journals of learned societies based in

London, Edinburgh, Calcutta, and Batavia, his *JIA* was, as C. M. Turnbull notes, 'the first attempt to promote a scientific periodical in the Straits Settlements' at a time when the Straits were considered by the British as little more than an obscure outpost of British India.[43]

Published between 1847 and 1862, the *JIA* went into 12 volumes and marked the first concerted effort to collect and compile ethnological, ethnographic, and philological information about East Asia and the Malay Peninsula, information that was to form the foundation of the ethnological collections at Singapore's first public library, the RLM, in 1874. In his 'prospectus', Logan conceived of the *JIA* as a means of connecting the Straits Settlement into a regional network of scientifically-focused useful knowledge societies that already spanned the Indian Ocean, taking in 'Calcutta, Madras, Bombay, Ceylon, and Hongkong', and regretting that the lack of such a society in the British Straits Settlements induced him to commence the *JIA*.[44] In contrast to the *SAQJ*, which was conceived as a means of connecting the Cape Colony to European and particularly British scientific networks and institutions, Logan sought to establish a regional network of European scientific researchers on the Indian Ocean, Southeast Asia, and the South Pacific that was genuinely transnational in character. In the 'prospectus', Logan is explicit about his debt to W. R. Barron von Hoëvell, President of the Batavian Society for Arts and Sciences and editor of the *Tijdschrift vor Neerlands Indie* (est. 1838), 'for his constant and most liberal assistance in making ourselves acquainted with the researches of himself and his countrymen'.[45] He states that one of the chief purposes of the *JIA* is to 'make English readers acquainted' with the researches of Dutch ethnologists and philologists in Indonesia.[46] However, it was not only the Dutch whose researches appeared in *JIA*. Contributors were French, German, Dutch, and Swiss, and even, in one instance, Chinese.[47] This was the first attempt to establish a trans-regional network of ethnological and philological researchers who would systematically collect, record, and disseminate ethnological, historical, and economic 'data' about the region.

The *JIA* elicited the majority of its contributions from the Straits Settlements' Anglophone professional and mercantile elites, and aspired to recognition from the global European scientific community.[48] Nearly a decade before British ethnologists Prichard and Richard Cull produced the first British ethnological questionnaire, Logan included a detailed 'Scheme of Desiderata' in the 'prospectus' to the *JIA* outlining guidance on the collection of ethnological data that was designed explicitly to shape the research agendas of these amateur gentlemen scientists.[49] The privileging of ethnological inquiry in Logan's 'Desiderata' is evinced by the fact that of the 22 subject categories suggested, 17 relate to 'human inhabitants'. Noting the historical underpinning of ethnological inquiry,[50] Logan nonetheless combines a qualitative, analytical, and distinctively humanistic mode of intellectual inquiry with a utilitarian concern with quantitative data: 'the reduction of every species of information that admits it, into an arithmetical or accurate quantitative form ... gives it a far greater value, both for practical and scientific purposes, than if it were merely stated in a loose or general manner'.[51] That Logan was at pains to ensure his amateur contributors provided information that was gathered using the most up-to-date scientific methodologies suggests that he aspired to a methodological rigour that would allow the *JIA* to maintain credibility within the broader international scientific community, rather than just being a journal of local interest.

As well as providing an important means of disseminating philological and ethnological researches conducted in Malaysia, Polynesia, and Oceania, and throughout the Anglo-world, to the metropolitan scientific establishment, Logan's *JIA* had a more lasting legacy. In 1874, the SL's assets were transferred to the new government-owned RLM. With a focus on acquiring works on East Asia, Malay manuscripts, and works of art, science, and literature, the RLM provided Singapore with its first publicly funded reference library. In 1878 the RLM purchased Logan's collection of ethnographic and philological books for £520, a move which, as Porscha Fermanis has argued, 'forever changed the character of the library's holdings'.[52] As Brendan Lyut points out, over the next 20 years the RLM consolidated its status as a regional 'centre of calculation ... for the South East Asian region' by purchasing collections of ethnographic material, such as that of Reinhold Rost, the former librarian to the India Office; supporting societies such as the Straits Branch of the Royal Asiatic Society and the Hakluyt Society; and increasingly purchasing scientific as well as literary periodicals.[53] 'All of these factors', as Fermanis notes, 'combined to create within the library a substantial archive of knowledge on the Malay Peninsula and its surrounding environs, which was only strengthened and supported by the establishment of the Straits Branch of the Royal Asiatic Society in 1877'.[54]

Initially housed in the RLM before moving to the adjacent Raffles Museum, the Straits Branch of the Royal Asiatic Society aimed 'to collect and record scientific information about the Malay Peninsula, and to carry out other scholarly activities including the publication of a journal and the formation of a library'.[55] Relying on the personal networks of its committee and members, and building its library collections primarily through donations and exchanges, the main focus of the Straits Branch of the Royal Asiatic Society was to build up regional networks of scientific scholarship and exchange publications with other scientific learned societies across Europe, India, East Asia, and Australia.[56] In this way, the Straits Branch of the Royal Asiatic Society provided the formal institutional framework to achieve what Logan had achieved informally through the *JIA*: the focusing of scholarly attention on British East India as a distinct geographical region.

Integral to the project of positioning itself as a centre for the collection and transmission of regional knowledge was the promotion of ethnological and philological scholarly inquiry. In 1878, at the inaugural meeting of the Straits Branch of the Royal Asiatic Society, Archdeacon F. R. Hose argued that Logan's ethnological papers published in the *JIA* 'will probably continue to be the most reliable authority upon the subject of those races which are, as usual, fast disappearing as civilization spreads inland'.[57] Mobilising an evolutionary rhetoric that mapped the biological determinism of Charles Darwin's *Origin of the Species* (1859) onto human societies, Hose argues that the extinction of Indigenous cultures was an inevitable process of the spread of European colonisation. The ethnological and philological insights about the Indigenous peoples of Southeast Asia and the Pacific that were published in the *JIA* retain value as a form of 'salvage ethnography', documenting the physical, linguistic, and cultural lives of Indigenous peoples rapidly vanishing under the dual pressures of colonial violence and acculturation. The society's interest in collecting and archiving the textual traces of these vanishing Indigenous cultures is evidenced by the fact that in 1879 it indexed Logan's *JIA*, and undertook the binding, labelling, and cataloguing of its own book collection in 1882, 1884, and 1890.[58]

'Knowing the Native Mind': Collecting and Classifying Indigenous Knowledge

The imbrication between philological and ethnological knowledge creation, collection, and transmission, and the project of 'moral colonisation' across the British Empire, is paradigmatically embodied in the figure of George Grey, whose colonial career took him across the southern colonies from South Australia to New Zealand via South Africa. At each stage of his career, as Donald Kerr has demonstrated, Grey was personally as well as politically invested in collecting, publishing, and, in his final years, archiving the textual traces of the languages and cultures of the Indigenous peoples he was required to govern.[59] Taken as a body, the knowledge collected by Grey and dispersed between the SAPL and the Auckland Public Library has been subject to contrasting historiographical interpretations. Kerr and Dubow view the donation of ethnological and philological collections as a manifestation of Grey's liberal support for public and intellectual institutions, and of his genuine interest in understanding Indigenous cultures, whereas Alan Lester views Grey's collections as the empirical legitimisation for a colonial policy increasingly aimed at enacting cultural genocide against the Indigenous inhabitants of Australia, South Africa, and New Zealand.[60]

What both readings of the Grey collections have in common is an acknowledgment that Grey viewed the act of ethnological and philological collecting as a form of 'rescue' or 'salvage'. The interest in collecting and conserving Indigenous languages emerged, as Hedley Twidle has argued, as an 'adjunct' to an interest in natural history.[61] This interest was cultivated by Grey while on a Royal Geographic Society-sponsored voyage of exploration on the north-west coast of Australia in 1837. During this expedition, Grey established himself as a major collector of natural historical information about north-western and western Australia, and his correspondence network reveals links to many prominent men of science of his day, including Darwin, Richard Owen, and Charles Lyell.[62] Grey's philological collecting began in earnest during 1839–1840, when he was employed as a Resident Magistrate in Albany, Western Australia. Here he collected and recorded language information on Indigenous groups in what was his first systematic attempt to collect and classify Indigenous languages: *The Vocabulary of the Dialects Spoken by the Aboriginal Races of S.W. Australia* (Albany, 1839), a publication whose trans-imperial reach was ensured by the printing of a London edition by T. and W. Boone in 1840.[63]

Grey's efforts to represent the languages of Australian and New Zealand Indigenous peoples in his philological publications are notable for being a rare example of a colonial governor undertaking the sort of in situ philological field work that was, in the earlier nineteenth century, most frequently undertaken by missionaries. Missionary linguistics and ethnography differed from the more scholarly projects of Orientalist comparative philology and philosophical ethnology in that it had a pedagogical function and was aimed primarily at communicative efficacy. As Rachel Leow has argued, missionary linguistics aimed at orthographic conventions that replicated the sound of the Indigenous language as far as possible in order to enable the missionary to 'communicate, proselytize, and persuade' Indigenous converts.[64] When Governor of New Zealand from 1845 to 1853, Grey had cultivated a transnational network of missionaries stationed throughout the British-controlled world from whom he was able to acquire a remarkable range of ethnological and philological materials that, due to their small print runs and ephemeral nature, would not have been available in conventional book markets.[65]

This network included George Augustus Selwyn, Bishop of New Zealand and founder of the Church Missionary Press at St. John's College, Auckland, as well as numerous missionaries of all denominations whose field of work stretched from New Zealand and the South Pacific, to Madagascar and western and southern Africa.[66] As Joseph Errington has argued, 'the intellectual work of writing speech was never entirely distinct from the "ideological" work of devising images of peoples in zones of colonial contact', and the written representations of Indigenous languages produced by missionaries and disseminated to a wide variety of reading publics across the Anglo-world through mission presses and publishing networks played a central role in the discursive formation of racial taxonomies throughout the nineteenth century.[67] As we shall see in the final section of this chapter, the grammars, catechisms, dictionaries, and word-lists amassed in Grey's philological collection at the SAPL were highly influential in shaping the classificatory schema for African languages devised by comparative philologist, and cataloguer and curator of the Grey collection, Wilhelm Bleek.

When Grey moved to Cape Town in 1854 to take up the governorship of the Cape Colony, his philological and ethnological collecting became both more extensive and more systematised. This began with the publication of *Books Wanted in the Library of His Excellency Sir. G. Grey, K.C.B.* (1855), a 12-page work that was sent to leading representatives of the six main missions working on the African continent requesting over 80 philological and pedagogical items in Indigenous languages produced by mission presses.[68] Between 1854 and 1861, Grey used the transnational networks cultivated during his time in Australia and New Zealand, as well as new links with missionary groups operating across the African continent, to amass an extensive collection of materials from sub-Saharan Africa, Indonesia, Australia, New Zealand, and the Pacific Islands. In 1861, Grey donated his substantial philological, ethnological, folklore, and antiquarian book collection to the SAPL.

The Grey collection operated on a number of symbolic levels. On the one hand, the antiquarian collection was 'intended to be seen as a "mirror of Western Culture"' to remind future generations of settler scholars of their European inheritance.[69] The donation of Grey's extensive collection of medieval manuscripts and early printed books also substantially raised the 'cultural capital' of the SAPL as an institution, boosting its credentials as a leading colonial research library. Yet more than Grey's antiquarian collection, what really put the SAPL on the map as a major research institution was Grey's decision to appoint the German comparative philologist Wilhelm Bleek as curator and compiler of the ethnological, philological, and folklore materials amassed by Grey and his networks. It was Bleek's philological researches and archiving of Indigenous 'Bushman' folklore that transformed the SAPL from a remote and relatively insignificant club of gentleman-scholars and recreational readers into a regional 'centre of calculation' for the collection, production, and global transmission of philological knowledge about southern Africa's Indigenous peoples. As Andrew Bank has noted, Bleek was both the first European intellectual to do anthropological field work in South Africa and 'the first systematic theorist of "race" in colonial South Africa'.[70]

Trained in classical philology at Bohn and Berlin, Rachael Gilmour has argued that Bleek was also the first to systematically apply the methodologies of classical philology as they had developed in Indo-European language study to the study of African languages, a methodology which 'conceived of [language] as a universal human phenomenon rooted in a regular and uniform developmental process'.[71] Furthermore, Bleek's philology was a product of the post-Darwinian turn in the natural and human sciences, and his classificatory schema for Indigenous languages differed from those developed by an earlier generation of pre-1860 comparative philologists 'in its explicitly evolutionary suppositions'.[72] The philological catalogues of Grey's collection that Bleek compiled were a pioneering attempt to apply evolutionary theory directly to the ethnographic study of the languages of the Indigenous peoples of southern Africa.

The Library of His Excellency Sir George Grey K.C.B.—Philology—South Africa was compiled by Bleek and published in 1858. Printed in Cape Town and distributed across Europe by Nicholas Trübner in London and F. A. Brockhaus in Leipzig, the catalogue consisted of 427 printed works and 78 manuscripts. Bleek's comparative philology of African languages rested on a typological system of classification based on grammatical gender in which he proposed two distinct classes of language: 'prefix-pronominal', in which the pronouns are originally borrowed from the derivative prefixes of the nouns, and 'sex denoting' or 'suffix-pronominal' languages, in which the pronouns are originally borrowed from the derivative suffixes to the nouns. Of particular significance is part one of the catalogue, which pertains to the 16 dialects spoken in southern Africa. In the case of South Africa, 'prefix-pronominal' languages included isiZulu, isiXhosa, siSwati, the Sotho-Tswana languages, and the Otjiherero language of Namibia. These languages were collectively given the ethno-linguistic classification 'Bantu' by Bleek. 'Suffix-pronominal' languages spoken in South Africa include Khoemana and all Khoisan languages; the Tonga language of Zambia and Zimbabwe; and the Nama language of Namibia. These were given the ethno-linguistic classification of 'Hottentot' and 'Bushman' languages by Bleek. By arguing that both Xhosa 'Kaffir' and San 'Bushman' languages were the most 'primitive forms' of the 'prefix-pronominal' and 'suffix-pronominal' language groups, Bleek's comparative philological project was deeply imbricated with contemporary anthropology and became highly influential in shaping European racial taxonomies.[73]

That Bleek intended his *South Africa* catalogue to constitute a major intervention in the field of comparative philology is evident from the extensive philological and ethnographic descriptions that precede the lists of works. These 'brief and lucid sketches' were described by an early reviewer in the *Cape Monthly Magazine* (est. 1851) as 'full of the most valuable and interesting information'.[74] The sources for Bleek's linguistic researches represented in the *South Africa* philological catalogue are generically diverse and historically extensive, encompassing voyages and travels dating as far back as the sixteenth century, contemporary ethnological works published in scientific journals, and, above all else, a diverse array of grammars, catechisms, spelling books, and primers published by the various mission presses operating across the southern part of the African continent. As well as developing a classificatory schema for African languages that he was also to apply to his catalogue of Grey's collection of materials on *Africa North of the Tropic of Capricorn* (1858), Bleek also documented the various orthographic conventions that had been adopted by European writers for denoting the 'clicks' in southern African languages. Throughout the catalogue, extensive bibliographic information on the size, extent, and place of publication as well as more qualitative remarks on the quality of the grammars and dictionaries provide further evidence of Bleek's extensive scholarly engagement with his materials.

Bleek built his philological career as an 'Africanist' working in South Africa as curator of the Grey collection, a position he held until his death in 1875. Yet his success in establishing himself as the foremost European expert in African philology was contingent upon the fact that he was a member of a European intellectual elite with connections to the heart of metropolitan Europe. His correspondence network included the leading ethnological and philological researchers in Britain and Germany, including Darwin, Lyell, Max Müller, Thomas Huxley, and Ernst Haeckel.[75] The compilation and distribution of the philological catalogues of the Grey collection undoubtedly did much to boost the prestige of Bleek's African philology in European intellectual circles. According to Kerr, two thirds of the 300-copy print run produced of the *South Africa* and *Africa* philology catalogues were sent to Trübner & Co. in London to be 'distributed according to Bleek's directions'. Accordingly, Trübner sent copies for review to notable London periodicals including the *Saturday Review*, *Notes and Queries*, the *Examiner*, and the *London Review*.[76] Copies were also sent to eminent European philologists including Professor Millies at Utrecht, Dr Haug at Bonn, and Dr Schleicher at Prague.[77] The distribution of the catalogues aided Grey in his task of acquiring materials, promoting the collection, and ensuring 'Grey's name became firmly associated with the collection of African language materials'.[78]

As well as the *South Africa* and *Africa* catalogues, Bleek compiled five philological catalogues documenting Grey's ethnological and philological collection of Australian, South Pacific, Madagascan, and New Zealand materials. The *Australia* and *New Zealand* catalogues are notable for the prestige given to Grey's own philological and ethnological writings; for example, the *New Zealand* catalogue includes the four compilations of Māori folklore, poetry, and proverbs that were collected by Grey and published during the 1850s, documents which constitute some of the earliest efforts to systematically record Māori orature.

In his 'introduction' to *Polynesian Mythology*, an English translation of a selection of Māori myths collected from Indigenous informants during his first period in New Zealand (1845–1853), Grey argues that both a mastery of the Māori language and the collection of their folklore were integral to achieving his political objectives as Governor of New Zealand:

> Clearly, however, I could not, as Governor of the country, permit so close a veil to remain drawn between myself and the aged and influential chiefs whom it was my duty to attach to British interests and to the British race ... Only one thing could under such circumstances be done, and that was to acquaint myself with the ancient language of the country, to collect its traditional poems and legends, to induce their priests to impart to me their mythology, and to study their proverbs.[79]

Philology and ethnology are explicitly conceived by Grey as tools of colonial governmentality, with mastery of Indigenous languages permitting clear communication with Indigenous leaders, and the collection of ethnological data on Indigenous cultures a means by which British administrators could study the 'native mind'. The ideological work done by such knowledge in the creation and formulation of categories of racial difference is well understood by critical anthropologists and imperial historians.[80] The role of Indigenous teachers such as Wiremu Maihi Te Rangikaheke (known as William Marsh), chief of the Rangiwewehi tribe of Rotorua, in imparting knowledge of Māori to Grey reveals the extent to which Indigenous cooperation and knowledge brokers were necessary to facilitate the sorts of intimate and sustained intercultural encounters that enabled imperial governors such as Grey to acquire this knowledge.[81]

Of the 87 items listed in the *Australia* catalogue, 17 grammars and vocabularies were authored by Grey himself.[82] One particular manuscript entry in the *Australia* catalogue gives an insight into Bleek and Grey's conception of ethnology and philology as a form of cultural salvage that, as Lester has argued, was a direct response to the material decline of Indigenous populations in Australia and across the British Empire that took place during Grey's tenures as Governor of South Australia and New Zealand.[83] Entry number 25, 'Two Songs of the Aborigines of Moreton Bay' in their original language and English translation collected by Grey, is glossed by Bleek with the following elegiac note:

> This is the only preserved specimen of a large collection of Australian Native Literature, destroyed by fire, when the Government House at Auckland, New Zealand, was burnt down;—an irreparable loss for science, since many of the tribes, represented in this collection, are now extinct.[84]

Such details when they surface in the Grey philological catalogues hint at another reading of the Grey archive. In spite of the efforts made by Grey and Bleek to classify and reify Indigenous knowledge into a textual archive legible and usable to European scholarship, the Grey philological archives, in Twidle's reading, 'point constantly to all that was never recorded, products of a colonial modernity that sought diligently–even lovingly–to record what it was in the process of destroying'.[85] In drawing the reader's attention to the material absences from the archive, such notes hint at the wider social process of 'genocide, forced acculturation and language death' that befell many of the Indigenous peoples whose language and orature was first documented by Bleek, Grey, and their trans-imperial network of Indigenous and European collaborators.[86]

As David Livingstone has argued, historians of science need to attend to the 'cultural geographies of science': the regionally specific cultures in which scientific knowledge is produced, discussed, and disseminated.[87] Far from just being sites in which ethnological and philological data on Indigenous peoples was gathered to be analysed and collated in metropolitan centres of collection and calculation,[88] public libraries, and the trans-imperial and trans-regional scientific networks cultivated therein, enabled colonial cities such as Melbourne, Singapore, and Cape Town to become regional centres of knowledge *creation*. Colonial scientists made a significant contribution to the formation of the bodies of ethnological and anthropological knowledge about the Indigenous peoples of Britain's colonies which, as the century progressed, increasingly influenced both British governmental policy and broader cultural attitudes amongst Europeans towards the Indigenous peoples of the expanding British Empire.

NOTES

1. Richard MacMahon, 'The History of Transdisciplinary Race Classification: Methods, Politics and Institutions, 1840s–1940s', *British Journal of History of Science* 51, no.1 (2018): 41–67 (66).
2. Macmahon, 'Transdisciplinary', 65.
3. Saul Dubow, *A Commonwealth of Knowledge: Science, Sensibility, and White South Africa, 1820–2000* (Oxford: Oxford University Press, 2006), 67.
4. Alan Lester, 'Settler Colonialism, George Grey and the Politics of Ethnography', *Environmental and Planning D: Society and Space* 34, no. 3 (2016): 492–507 (493).
5. *Catalogue*, SAPL, 1825: http://www.ucd.ie/southhem/record.html#261; *Catalogue*, SAPL, 1829: http://www.ucd.ie/southhem/record.html#264; *Catalogue*, SAPL, 1834: http://www.ucd.ie/southhem/record.html#266; *Catalogue*, SAPL, 1842: http://www.ucd.ie/southhem/record.html#269; *Catalogue*, SAPL, 1862: http://www.ucd.ie/southhem/record.html#270; *Catalogue*, SALMI, 1848: http://www.ucd.ie/southhem/record.html#49; *Catalogue*, SALMI, 1851: http://www.ucd.ie/southhem/record.html#77; SAI, 1861: http://www.ucd.ie/southhem/record.html#113; *Catalogue*, SAI, with first supplement, 1863: http://www.ucd.ie/southhem/record.html#124; *Catalogue*, SAI, 1869: http://www.ucd.ie/southhem/record.html#188; *Catalogue*, ASL, 1839: http://www.ucd.ie/southhem/record.html#30; *Catalogue*, ASL, 1843: http://www.ucd.ie/southhem/record.

html#33; *Catalogue*, ASL, 1853: http://www.ucd.ie/southhem/record.html#520; *Catalogue*, SL, 1860: http://www.ucd.ie/southhem/record.html#109; *Catalogue*, SL, 1863: http://www.ucd.ie/southhem/record.html#131.
6. Sadiah Qureshi, *Peoples on Parade: Exhibitions, Empire and Anthropology in Nineteenth-Century Britain* (Chicago: University of Chicago Press, 2011), 212.
7. Macmahon, 'Transdisciplinary', 48.
8. B. Ricardo Brown, *Until Darwin: Science, Human Variety and the Origins of Race* (London: Pickering and Chatto, 2010), 17.
9. Some colonial libraries such as the SL and the SAPL even classified 'voyages and travels' as a sub-category of 'history'. See, for example, SL, 1863: http://www.ucd.ie/southhem/record.html#131; SAPL, 1862: http://www.ucd.ie/southhem/record.html#270.
10. *General Catalogue of Bound Volumes in the Raffles Library*, Sept. 1st, 1877 (Singapore: s.n., 1877), n.p.
11. Macmahon, 'Transdisciplinary', 47.
12. *Catalogue*, SAPL, 1862: http://www.ucd.ie/southhem/record.html#270.
13. *Catalogue*, SAPL, 1829: http://www.ucd.ie/southhem/record.html#264; *Catalogue*, SAPL, 1834: http://www.ucd.ie/southhem/record.html#266; *Catalogue*, SAPL, 1842: http://www.ucd.ie/southhem/record.html#269.
14. *Catalogue*, SAPL, 1842, 88: http://www.ucd.ie/southhem/record.html#269.
15. *Catalogue*, MPL, 1858, portion two: http://www.ucd.ie/southhem/record.html#543.
16. On the disciplinary formation of ethnology in the 1840s and 1850s, see, for example, George W. Stocking, *Victorian Anthropology* (New York: Free Press, 1987); Sadiah Qureshi, 'Robert Gordon Latham, Displayed Peoples, and the Natural History of Race, 1854–1866', *The Historical Journal* 54, no. 1 (March 2011): 143–166; Macmahon, 'Transdisciplinary', 46–48.
17. 'Polygenesis' refers to the belief that humanity is descended from more than one original pair of individuals. 'Monogenesis', in line with the Biblical interpretation of creation, is the belief that all humanity is descended from a single pair of individuals.
18. Qureshi, 'Gordon', 162.
19. *Catalogue*, SAPL, 1862: http://www.ucd.ie/southhem/record.html#270; *Catalogue*, MPL, 1861: http://www.ucd.ie/southhem/record.html#112; *Catalogue*, SAI, 1869, http://www.ucd.ie/southhem/record.html#188.
20. *Catalogue*, MPL, 1865: http://www.ucd.ie/southhem/record.html#147.
21. Wallace Kirsop, 'German Science in Nineteenth-Century Australian Libraries', *The Royal Society of Victoria* 127 (2015): 39–42 (41).
22. John Dunham, 'The British India Holdings of the State Library of Victoria', *La Trobe Journal* 16 (1975): 77–88 (81).

23. *Catalogue*, MPL, 1861: http://www.ucd.ie/southhem/record.html#112. While the classificatory index for the MPL separates these categories, some of the authors are listed repeatedly in multiple categories. Many authors listed under 'Philology' are also found under 'Travels & Voyages', for example.
24. *Catalogue*, MPL, 1865: http://www.ucd.ie/southhem/record.html#147.
25. *Catalogue*, SAI, 1869: http://www.ucd.ie/southhem/record.html#188.
26. Efram Sera-Shriar, 'Ethnology in the Metropole: Robert Knox, Robert Gordon Latham and Local Sites of Observational Training', *Studies in History and Philosophy of Biological and Biomedical Sciences* 42 (2011): 486–496 (487).
27. *Andrew Smith's Journal of His Expedition into the Interior of South Africa, 1834–36*, ed. William F. Lye (Cape Town: A. A. Balkema, 1975), 3.
28. On the interrelationship between the practice of medicine and the development of British ethnology, see Sera-Shriar, 'Ethnology in the Metropole', 487.
29. *Catalogue*, SAPL, 1826: http://www.ucd.ie/southhem/record.html#449.
30. On the contemporary reception of Lawrence's work in 1820s Britain, see Peter G. Mudford, 'William Lawrence and The Natural History of Man', *Journal of the History of Ideas* 29, no. 3 (1968): 430–436.
31. *Catalogue*, SAPL, 1826: http://www.ucd.ie/southhem/record.html#449.
32. *Catalogue*, SAPL, 1829: http://www.ucd.ie/southhem/record.html#264; *Catalogue*, SAPL, 1825: http://www.ucd.ie/southhem/record.html#261.
33. *Catalogue*, SAPL, 1829: http://www.ucd.ie/southhem/record.html#264.
34. Dubow, *Commonwealth of Knowledge*, 44.
35. Jon Mee, 'A Reading People?: Global Knowledge Networks and Two Australian Societies of the 1820s', *Australian Literary Studies* 29, no.3 (2015): 74–86.
36. *South African Quarterly Journal* 1, no.1 (1829): 3.
37. Leigh Davin Bregman, '"Snug Little Coteries": A History of Scientific Societies in Early Nineteenth Century Cape Town, 1824–1835' (PhD diss, University College London, England, 2001), 133.
38. Bregman, '"Snug Little Coteries"', 123.
39. James Cowles Prichard, 'Anniversary Address for 1848, to the Ethnological Society of London on the Recent Progress of Ethnology', *Journal of the Ethnological Society of London* 2 (1850): 119.
40. Qureshi, *Peoples on Parade*, 86.
41. *The Sixth Report of the Singapore Library 1850* (Singapore: Singapore Free Press Office, 1850), 10; *The Seventh Report of the Singapore Library 1851* (Singapore: Singapore Free Press Office, 1851), 7.
42. *Straits Times* (Singapore), September 30, 1846, 3.
43. C. M. Turnball, 'James Richardson Logan', *Oxford Dictionary of National Biography*, accessed June 5, 2018: https://doi.org/10.1093/ref:odnb/16941.

44. J. R. Logan, 'Prospectus of *The Journal of the Indian Archipelago and Eastern Asia*' (Singapore, n.s., 1847), iv.
45. Logan, 'Prospectus', vi.
46. Logan, 'Prospectus', iv.
47. G. F. Hose, 'Inaugural address by the President, the Venerable Archdeacon Hose, M. A. Delivered on the 28th February 1878', *Journal of the Straits Branch of the Royal Asiatic Society* 1 (1878): 3. The sole Chinese contributor was Seah Eu Chin, a prominent merchant and leader in the Chinese community in Singapore, *JIA* 2 (1848): 283–289.
48. Hose, 'Inaugural address', 3.
49. On ethnological questionnaires and the observational practices of nineteenth-century British ethnologists, see Efram Sera-Shriar, 'What is Armchair Anthropology? Observational Practices in 19th-Century British Human Sciences', *History of Human Sciences* 27, no. 2 (2014): 29.
50. Logan, 'Prospectus', 5.
51. Logan, 'Prospectus', 5.
52. Porscha Fermanis, 'British Cultures of Reading and Literary Appreciation in Nineteenth-Century Singapore', in *The Edinburgh History of Reading: A World Survey from Antiquity to Present*, ed. Mary Hammond and Jonathan Rose (Edinburgh: Edinburgh University Press), forthcoming 2019, n.p.
53. Brendan Luyt, 'Centres of Calculation and Unruly Colonists: The Colonial Library in Singapore and its Users, 1874–1900', *Journal of Documentation* 64, no. 3 (2008): 386–396 (391). On Rost's collection of mainly philological books, see *Catalogue of the Rost Collection in the Raffles Library Singapore* (Singapore: Printed at the American Mission Press, 1897).
54. Fermanis, 'British Cultures of Reading', n.p.
55. Fermanis, 'British Cultures of Reading', n.p; 'Proceedings of the Straits Branch of the Royal Asiatic Society', *Journal of the Straits Branch of the Royal Asiatic Society* 1 (1878): iii–ix (iv, iii, ix).
56. Fermanis, 'British Cultures of Reading', n.p. See the list of exchanges in *Journal of the Straits Branch of the Royal Asiatic Society* 24 (1882): xvii–xviii.
57. Hose, 'Inaugural address', 4.
58. N. B. Dennys, 'A Contribution to Malayan Bibliography', *Journal of the Straits Branch of the Royal Asiatic Society* 5 (1880): 69–123; E. M. Santow, 'Essay Towards a Bibliography of Siam', *Journal of the Straits Branch of the Royal Asiatic Society* 17 (1886): 1–86. See also *Catalogue of the Logan Library* (Singapore: Straits Times Press, 1880).
59. For a comprehensive account of George Grey's natural historical, philological, ethnological, and antiquarian book collecting, see Donald Jackson Kerr, '"Building Monuments More Enduring than Brass": Governor Sir George Grey, A Study of his Book Collection and the Formation of his Libraries'

(PhD, University of Auckland, 2001). This chapter has drawn extensively on Kerr's exhaustively researched thesis, and his subsequent monograph, *Amassing Treasures for All Time: Sir George Grey, Colonial Bookman and Collector* (Dunedin, NZ and New Castle, DE: Otago University Press, 2006), for much of the information that follows on Grey's collection and publication practices, and his correspondence networks.
60. Lester, 'Settler Colonialism', 495.
61. Hedley Twidle, 'From *The Origin of Language* to a Language of Origin: A Prologue to the Grey Collection', in *Print, Text and Book Cultures in South Africa*, ed. Andrew van der Vlies (Johannesburg: Wits University Press, 2012), 252–283 (254).
62. Kerr, '"Building Monuments More Enduring than Brass"', 136.
63. Kerr, '"Building Monuments More Enduring than Brass"', 153.
64. Rachel Leow, *Taming Babel: Language and the Making of Malaysia* (Cambridge: Cambridge University Press, 2016), 71.
65. On Grey's collaborations with a range of Indigenous teachers and informants, see Kerr, '"Building Monuments More Enduring than Brass"', 196–197; and Jenifer Curnow, 'Wiremu Maihi Te Rangikahekeke: His Life and Work', *The Journal of the Polynesian Society* 94, no. 2 (1985), 97–147.
66. Kerr, '"Building Monuments More Enduring than Brass"', 244.
67. Joseph Errington, *Linguistics in a Colonial World: A Story of Language, Meaning and Power* (Malden MA and Oxford: Blackwell, 2008), 5. See also Rachael Gilmour, *Grammars of Colonialism: Representing Languages in Colonial South Africa* (Basingstoke: Palgrave, 2006).
68. Kerr, '"Building Monuments More Enduring than Brass"', 309.
69. Dubow, *Commonwealth of Knowledge*, 67.
70. Andrew Bank, 'Evolution and Racial Theory: The Hidden Side of Wilhelm Bleek', *South African Historical Journal* 43, no. 1 (2000): 163–178 (163).
71. Gilmour, *Grammars of Colonialism*, 192.
72. Gilmour, *Grammars of Colonialism*, 193.
73. Gilmour, *Grammars of Colonialism*, 188.
74. *Cape Monthly Magazine* 3 (June 1858): 321.
75. Robert Thornton, 'Narrative Ethnography in Africa, 1850–1920: The Creation and Capture of an Appropriate Domain for Anthropology', *Man* 18, no.3 (1983): 502–50 (502); Gilmour, *Grammars of Colonialism*, 171.
76. Kerr, '"Building Monuments More Enduring than Brass"', 345.
77. Kerr, '"Building Monuments More Enduring than Brass"', 346.
78. Kerr, '"Building Monuments More Enduring than Brass"', 348.
79. Quoted in Kerr, '"Building Monuments More Enduring than Brass"', 193.
80. See, for example, Johannes Fabian, *Language and Colonial Power: The Appropriation of Swahili in the Former Belgian Congo, 1880–1938* (New York and Cambridge: Cambridge University Press, 1986); Anne L. Stoler,

Carnal Knowledge and Imperial Power: Race and the Invention of Colonial Rule (Berkeley: University of California Press, 2002); Errington, *Linguistics in a Colonial World*.

81. A letter by Te Rangikaheke evidences a close relationship between the two, with Te Rangikeheke living with the Greys. For more see, Jennifer Curnow, 'Wiremu Maihi Te Rangikahekeke'.
82. *The Library of His Excellency Sir George Grey KCB – Philology – Australia* (Cape Town: G. J. Pike, 1858).
83. Lester, 'Settler Colonialism', 497.
84. *The Library of His Excellency Sir George Grey KCB*, 26.
85. Hedley Twidle, '"The Bushmen's Letters": |Xam Narratives of the Bleek Lloyd Archive and their Afterlives', in *The Cambridge History of South African Literature*, ed. David Attwell and Derek Attridge (Cambridge: Cambridge University Press, 2012), 19–37 (37).
86. Twidle, '"The Bushman's Letters"', 37.
87. David N. Livingstone, *Putting Science in its Place: Geographies of Scientific Knowledge* (Chicago: University of Chicago Press, 2003), 108.
88. Bruno Latour, *Science in Action: How to Follow Scientists and Engineers through Society* (Cambridge MA: Harvard, 1988), 237.

Open Access This chapter is licensed under the terms of the Creative Commons Attribution 4.0 International License (http://creativecommons.org/licenses/by/4.0/), which permits use, sharing, adaptation, distribution and reproduction in any medium or format, as long as you give appropriate credit to the original author(s) and the source, provide a link to the Creative Commons licence and indicate if changes were made.

The images or other third party material in this chapter are included in the chapter's Creative Commons licence, unless indicated otherwise in a credit line to the material. If material is not included in the chapter's Creative Commons licence and your intended use is not permitted by statutory regulation or exceeds the permitted use, you will need to obtain permission directly from the copyright holder.

CHAPTER 6

Conclusion

Abstract This conclusion considers the roles that colonial public libraries played in a wider imperial context, focusing on their contribution to a global 'civilising' process and to the emergence of an economic world system of goods, capital, and people. Looking also at the role of public libraries in educating the working classes and the youth of the colonies, it argues that these libraries were part of a larger programme of civic education that sought to define a new type of egalitarian colonial citizenry. It ends by providing a comparative summary of the case study libraries under discussion, as well as contextualising these libraries within developments relating to library provision in nineteenth-century America, Britain, and British India.

Keywords Imperialism • Citizenship • Education • Public libraries
• British India

The inauguration in 1860 of the neoclassical building that currently houses the SAPL took place against the political backdrop of the visit to the Cape Colony of Prince Alfred, Queen Victoria's second son. Keen to exploit the symbolic capital embodied in the visit by the emissary of the 'centre of Christianity and of civilization' to 'the extremity of this ancient continent, which was the cradle of civilization and art', the Cape Colony's Governor, Sir George Grey, used the occasion to argue for the centrality of the SAPL in particular, and the Cape Colony more broadly, to the work of the British Empire on the African continent.[1]

Grey's historiographical framing of the SAPL in his address situates southern Africa's foremost nineteenth-century research library in a genealogy of civilising institutions on the African continent that dates back to the foundation of the first library at Alexandria as a 'seat of Christianity and civilization' in the midst of the 'ignorance, sloth, and barbarism' that, according to Grey, characterised the cultural and intellectual lives of sub-Saharan Africa's Indigenous populations when unmoored from the benevolent influence of Christian colonisers and their political and cultural institutions.[2] While in the Cape Colony this historical narrative followed the Manichean logic of hardening colonial racism, public libraries in the Australian colonies also framed themselves as 'institutions for the safety and security of our national progress' and 'tools for the spreading of civilization'.[3] In the Straits Settlements, the rhetoric surrounding the Singapore Institution, and its related free school and library, similarly imagined it both as a local 'source of information and enlightenment to the neighbouring states and stations' from Siam to Sarawak, and as a more general 'beacon' within a larger British Empire.[4]

The belief that a public library was part of a global 'civilising' process linked to the wider functions and practices of empire was in many ways associated with the special role that missionaries and evangelical groups had played in establishing reading and print cultures in the colonies, but it also reflected the evangelising tendencies of nineteenth-century imperialism more generally. Sir George Grey, whose gubernatorial career in the southern colonies was inseparable from the evangelically-inflected Anglicanism that underpinned it, explicitly argued that the SAPL was the symbolic manifestation of the attempt 'boldly entered' into by Britain 'of establishing civilization and Christianity in this continent, and of spreading their blessings through the boundless territories which lie beyond our [colonial] borders'.[5]

Grey's speech exemplifies how the inauguration ceremonies of colonial public libraries were seized upon by colonial administrators as public opportunities to present their emergent national narratives on a world stage. Addressing themselves to a global Anglophone audience, the oratorical performances of colonial governors on these occasions enabled them to argue for the central role of their colonies in the British imperial world system that, as the nineteenth century progressed, was characterised by increasing intra-imperial competition as each colony sought to capitalise on the mass transfers of emigrants, capital, and goods that flowed across the British Empire.

At the laying of the foundation for a new public library building in Adelaide in 1879, Governor Sir W. F. Drummond Jervois, previously Governor of the Straits Settlements from 1875 to 1877 and future Governor of New Zealand from 1883 to 1888, was equally keen to emphasise the interconnection between the role of the public library as a publicly accessible reference library facilitating 'the satisfactory pursuit of study' and the broader economic life of the colony.[6] Drummond Jervois's speech links the free diffusion of knowledge across the social world of the settler colony with the opening of new economic, geographical, and extractive frontiers:

> It is most important that the Library should contain works bearing on discoveries in physical science and the industrial arts, particularly those referring most directly to the unfolding and opening up of the natural and artificial resources of new countries.[7]

In this rhetorical doubling, the industrious student in the reference library is as much a part of the economic fabric of the colony as the gold and copper mines that had, by 1876, sprung up in the hills and mountains surrounding Adelaide. This link between the intellectual and mineral resources of the colony is also mobilised by Grey through the metaphor of the mine. The SAPL is 'a great mine for all South Africa, in which is treasured up the wealth acquired by many mighty minds of various races and of many ages, which may be consulted free of cost by all students who may resort to it'.[8] In both these cases, free access to knowledge provides the cultural capital and practical expertise that enables wealth creation and territorial expansion.

The centrality of scientific and industrial knowledge to the colony's economic survival was framed by Drummond Jervois in the Darwinian language of global and regional intra-colonial competition. Recognising that 'technological movement is greatly extending its influence in all civilized nations', he views the public library as a means of placing responsibility for technological innovation, and working-class education, in the hands of an (implicitly middle-class) colonial citizenry rather than state institutions: 'it behoves you to use every reasonable effort to place at the disposal of your artisans information bearing on the industrial occupations which are so intimately connected with your present and future welfare'.[9] Only by collectively disseminating knowledge and technological innovations to an industrious artisanal class can South Australia be adequately equipped to win the 'race' 'you will have to run in the future—not only with foreign countries but with even your neighbours on this continent'.[10]

That Drummond Jervois viewed South Australia as ready to compete not only with the other Australian colonies but also with industrial Europe indicates the accelerated pace at which the southern colonies had modernised during the period 1820–1880. With their unique opportunities for upward social mobility and their relatively high levels of literacy, the motivation for the establishment of public libraries in colonial societies was not confined to the need to replicate and 'keep pace' with the institutions of the 'old country'. Such libraries were also seen as a way of promoting and maximising the potential of emerging 'young countries' by disseminating knowledge and encouraging life-long learning.

Reporting on the ceremony opening the Sydney FPL on 30 September 1869, the *Sydney Morning Herald* printed verbatim the Earl of Belmore's inauguration address, which argued that the FPL would help to remedy the 'disadvantage' of those 'whose early education has been neglected, or whose means of purchasing books have been limited':

> In these colonies the highest positions are open to all who are qualified by education and ability to fill them; and, although it may rarely happen that a total want of early education can be in after-life supplied, yet it cannot be doubted that this institution may be the means of doing much in furtherance of the endeavours of those who may be trying to remedy such a want, as well as of those more fortunate persons, who only seek to keep up and increase that knowledge which they have acquired in the period of youth.[11]

Of particular interest here is not just the implicit invocation of a continuous life-cycle of learning, but also the sense of how a specifically colonial egalitarianism could aid in that continuous learning. Yet for all its rhetorical commitment to what appear to be meritocratic principles of universal access to education, it must also be borne in mind that the FPL's utilitarian imperative towards self-improvement and continuous learning was balanced by a strategic policing of the boundaries between improving and frivolous knowledge. At the same moment that the Earl of Belmore acknowledged that the Sydney FPL was an integral part of the colony's education system, John Dunmore Lang, a former proprietor of the ASL, noted that the FPL would focus upon acquiring non-fiction books 'likely to afford instruction to the public at large' rather than fiction which was deemed 'of little use to the community'.[12]

Library committee men throughout the southern colonies and Straits Settlements therefore conceived of the role of a public library as both an opportunity to aid the progress of the 'march of the intellect' across the colonies through the free diffusion of knowledge and as a means of directing the young and the working classes towards educative information that would further the economic and cultural agendas already set by their social superiors. At the opening of the SAI, Rowland Rees, chairman of the Board of Governors, defined the purpose of the continuous learning facilitated by free public libraries as 'the utilization and development of all the powers of men for the best purpose, adding to the productiveness of industry ... the wealth-producing power ... the improvements in inventive skill ... [and] the fostering of character, economy, morality, and social influence'.[13] In this marrying of egalitarian idealism and economic instrumentalism, the patrons and administrators of the public libraries of the southern colonies positioned their institutions at the centre of a capacious programme of civic education that aimed to mould the intellectual, social, and economic lives of an increasingly assertive colonial citizenry.

The rhetorical and ideological similarities between these three speeches are suggestive of shared attitudes towards early public library culture and provision across the southern colonies. At the same time, however, this study has shown that the specifics of that provision differed considerably in each jurisdiction. In the case of the Cape Colony, the example of the free-to-access Dessinian Collection, which followed a relatively well-developed tradition of freely accessible reference libraries in Joachim Nicolaas von Dessin's native Germany, is likely to have been influential in the establishment of the SAPL.[14] In the decade preceding the granting of limited self-rule to the Cape Colony in 1854, the SAPL committee foregrounded the library's role as part of a cluster of colonial educational institutions aimed at honing the intellectual and moral sensibilities of its citizens.

In the same period, the MPL was similarly linked to a 'consortium' or 'loose confederation' of institutions—including the Supreme Court and University of Melbourne—celebrating the colony of Victoria's independence after its separation from New South Wales in 1851 and the achievement of responsible government in 1854.[15] At the joint laying of the foundation stones of the MPL and the University of Melbourne in 1854, the Speaker of the Legislative Council, Dr Palmer, identified these institutions as the 'quarry' from 'which students would draw the material with which to store their minds with useful and varied knowledge', making explicit the link between the intellectual improvement provided by the MPL and the civic development of the colony as a whole.[16] In New South Wales, on the other hand, the establishment of the Sydney FPL in 1869 was hindered rather than helped by a notoriously elitist local government. While from the 1870s onwards municipal rate-funded libraries were established in greater numbers in the Australian colonies than elsewhere, relatively few survived into the twentieth century.[17] The TPL is an outlying example of a comparatively large, rate-supported municipal library in nineteenth-century colonial Australia.

In Singapore and the rest of the Straits Settlements, library development was more haphazard and uncoordinated. From 1833 until 1867, the British administration in Calcutta actively pursued a policy of non-intervention in the Straits. Until the establishment of the RLM in 1874, libraries and schools were funded primarily by a combination of private initiatives, missionary interventions, and small 'grants-in-aid'.[18] In contrast, public library provision in British India has been described as 'far [a]head of contemporary thinking on these issues worldwide'.[19] By the first half of the nineteenth century, the three presidency towns each had a public library of sorts. While the Madras Literary Society (est. 1818), the Bombay General Library (est. 1820), and the Calcutta Public Library (est. 1836) all retained membership fees, they also had a policy that permitted free access to students and 'respectable strangers visiting the City'.[20] Early nineteenth-century library provision in India was therefore characterised by a relative openness that was increasingly replicated in the southern colonies. While library management committees in all jurisdictions were primarily composed of white, male, middle-class professionals, access provisions and opening hours were notably more relaxed than in Britain.

Priya Joshi's list of available authors of British fiction held across libraries in nineteenth-century India suggests a significant overlap with the best-stocked authors in the SAPL and RLM, including Bulwer-Lytton, Scott, Dickens, Marryat, and James.[21] These authors were also popular in Britain, reflecting not only the provenance of most of the books in the public libraries of the southern colonies, but also publishing distribution practices and agents' selection policies.[22] By the 1850s, the SL, for example, was getting its books primarily from Mudie's Circulating Library, which itself stocked books (mainly fiction) intended for conservative middle-class audiences. Experienced colonial agents and/or publishers based in London, such as J. M. Richardson and Smith, Elder & Co. tended either to promote their own books or to distribute books and series from publishers such as Henry Colburn and Richard Bentley, themselves prevalent on the shelves of British circulating libraries.

Given the popularity of fiction among subscribers, libraries that retained the user-pays subscription model were more likely to hold higher proportions of fiction and lower proportions of science, history, and biography. As a subscription library with demanding members, the SAI defended its level of fiction holdings and its role as a provider of entertainment, arguing more forcefully than the other libraries for the utility-value of fiction. The SAPL, MPL, and FPL, on the other hand, held significantly less prose fiction, reflecting their status as serious reference libraries. The MPL and FPL went further than the other colonial public libraries in limiting their novels to 'edifying' authors such as Edgeworth, Scott, Disraeli, and Richardson. By 1871, the Melbourne *Age* reported that the MPL contained 'only about 300 volumes of light literature and fiction' and relatively few periodicals.[23]

Attitudes towards archiving local print and manuscript material differed considerably across the southern colonies. In Singapore and Cape Town, where there were either significant Indigenous populations or large non-white diasporic populations from China, India, and the Malay Archipelago, there was a more concerted effort to collect the results of ethnographic field work. In the case of both the RLM and the SAPL, large donations and bequests of ethnographic materials by the gentleman ethnographers James Richardson Logan and George Grey were important catalysts for both the collection of ethnographic knowledge and its production. Grey's appointment in 1856 of the eminent German comparative philologist Wilhelm Bleek as the librarian and cataloguer of his collection at the SAPL was a conscious effort to put African philology on the disciplinary map of the European scientific establishment. Meanwhile, the RLM's 1878 purchase of Logan's ethnological and philological book collection, and its close relationship with the Straits Branch of the Royal Asiatic Society, gradually transformed the RLM into a regional centre for the collection of ethnographic material on the Indigenous peoples of Southeast Asia.

Despite Redmond Barry's interest in comparative philology and Aboriginal languages, this archiving of Indigenous knowledge production was not replicated either at the MPL or any of the other public libraries in colonial Australia in the 1850s, 1860s, and 1870s, pointing to different attitudes towards so-called salvage ethnography, as well as to diverse understandings of the role of the public library in fostering colonial 'national self-purpose'.[24] Collections of local settler pamphlets, books, and manuscripts, and of material relating to particular regions, were also more assiduously pursued in Cape Town and Singapore between 1840 and 1880. In contrast to these libraries and to libraries in Britain, the collection and archiving of local material was more haphazard in the Australian colonies. In Melbourne, the first purchase of Australian manuscript material by the library (as opposed to donations or bequests) did not occur until 1913, and it was not until the mid-twentieth century that a real commitment to the archiving of Australian materials was established.[25]

In terms of library users, attitudes towards women and the working classes were consistent across all the libraries in the southern colonies, but the most trenchant was the MPL, which perceived its opening hours and open access policy to be particularly attractive to loafers and loungers, and hence imposed high standards of dress, behaviour, and cleanliness. While the number of loafers who frequented the MPL was probably small, the library was nonetheless frequently ridiculed by colonial newspapers for becoming a haven for vagrants, who wished simply to escape inclement weather. The creation of a ladies' room in 1859 was mostly viewed in a positive light as encouraging respectable behaviour within the library's walls and consequently discouraging the disreputable loafers. Women readers were nonetheless frequently associated with light and frivolous reading. The RLM was the only library to explicitly contemplate its use by non-white readers in the nineteenth century, and had at least one prominent Chinese businessman on its management committee, as well as a small number of Malay, Chinese, and Indian subscribers. In Cape Town and the Australian colonies, on the other hand, Indigenous readers were mainly served by mission libraries. The lack of involvement of Indigenous populations in the establishment and use of public libraries in the southern hemisphere colonies differs considerably from the example of British India, where, as Joshi has noted, the Calcutta Public Library was 'expressly set up with the fiscal, political, and ideological collaboration between Indians and the British'.[26] While to some extent this was the result of the demographic profiles of the Presidency towns with their large Indian populations and small British administrative class, such collaborations were not always realised in other franchise colonies with large Indigenous or non-European populations, such as the Cape Colony.

While the effect of the British *Public Libraries Act* was palpable on the emergence of public libraries in the southern colonies in the 1850s and 1860s, in many ways early public library provision in colonial Australia, Southeast Asia, and South Africa more closely follows developments in British India than in Britain or America. As in India, many of the most important public libraries in the southern colonies evolved from volunteer or community attempts to amalgamate or extend subscription libraries (for example, the FPL and RLM) and mechanics' institutes (for example, the SAI), or from government grants canvased by prominent community members (for example, the MPL) rather than from centralised municipal legislation, which was enacted in Australia, the Cape Colony, and Singapore in the 1860s and 1870s with mixed results. In America, on the other hand, legislation in the 1850s enabled free libraries on a town level in a handful of states, rising to around 188 municipal libraries by 1876.[27]

Like their metropolitan counterparts, colonial public libraries in the British southern hemisphere and Straits Settlements in the 1870s and 1880s were important but still relatively isolated examples of a new liberal emphasis on the provision of 'civilising' and self-improving educational opportunities for the working classes and, to a lesser extent, Indigenous populations. Despite claims that libraries like the MPL were more like 'a magnificent library of a private mansion' than 'an institute for the people',[28] these libraries were a source of pride and civic empowerment for their communities, feeding into debates about self-governance, federation, and responsible government, as well as being part of the growth of a wider publicly funded civic infrastructure that reflected the developing maturity of colonial states. Most obviously, such libraries were influential in shaping questions of incipient 'national' identities, but they were also important communicative institutions, influencing and regulating public discourse by deciding what information was made available to the public and which groups were involved in their participatory mechanisms. They therefore played a formative role in shaping colonial public discourse in the nineteenth century, contributing to broader public-sphere debates on questions of race, self-governance, and imperial citizenship, and helping to instantiate ideologies of productive work and improving leisure that were increasingly central to the self-definition of the 'modern' colonial states in which they were situated.

Notes

1. *Inauguration of the New Buildings Erected for the South African Public Library and Museum, by His Royal Highness Prince Alfred. 18th September 1860* (Cape Town: Saul Solomon, 1860), 4.
2. *Inauguration*, 5–6.
3. *The South Australian Institute: Comprising the Public Library, Art Gallery, and Museums. Addresses Delivered at the Laying of the Foundation* (Adelaide: W. K. Thomas and Co., 1879), 11.
4. *The Report of the Singapore Institution Free Schools for the Year 1856–57* (Singapore: Straits Times Press by G. M. Frederick, 1858), 10.

5. *Inauguration*, 6.
6. *South Australian Institute*, 14.
7. *South Australian Institute*, 15.
8. *Inauguration*, 8.
9. *South Australian Institute*, 16–17.
10. *South Australian Institute*, 17.
11. *Sydney Morning Herald*, October 1, 1869, 5.
12. *Sydney Morning Herald*, October 1, 1869, 5.
13. *South Australian Institute*, 6.
14. See Hans G. Schulte-Albert, 'Gottfried Wilhelm Leibniz and Library Classification', *The Journal of Library History (1966–1972)* 6, no. 2 (1971): 133–152.
15. Sue Reynolds, 'Libraries, Librarians, and Librarianship in the Colony of Victoria', *Australian Academic and Research Libraries* 40, no. 1 (2013): 50–64 (59).
16. *Argus* (Melbourne), July 4, 1854, 4.
17. See, for example, David J. Jones, 'Public Library Development in New South Wales', *The Australian Library Journal* 54, no. 2 (2003): 130–137.
18. Edward Lim Huck Tee, *Libraries in West Malaysia and Singapore* (Kuala Lumpur: University of Malaya Library, 1970), 12.
19. Jashu Patel and Krishan Kumar, *Libraries and Librarianship in India* (Westport CN: Greenwood Press), 9; *Singapore Free Press and Mercantile Advertiser*, August 24, 1843, 2.
20. *East India Company Board's Collection* 1838–1839, 20, quoted in Priya Joshi, *In Another County: Colonialism, Culture and the English Novel in India* (New York: Columbia University Press, 2002), 46.
21. Joshi, *In Another Country*, 64.
22. For popular authors, see Richard Altick, *The English Common Reader: A Social History of the Mass Reading Public, 1800–1900* (Chicago: University of Chicago Press, 1957), Appendices B and C. For importation and distribution practices in the Australian colonies, see Graeme Johanson, *A Study of Colonial Editions in Australia, 1843–1972* (Wellington: Elibank Press, 2000).
23. *Age* (Melbourne), June 17, 1871, quoted in David McVilly, '"Something to Blow About"?—the State Library of Victoria, 1856–1880', *La Trobe Journal* 8 (1971): 81–90 (86). The FPL retained selected works of prose fiction in its reference collection but they were not available for borrowing.
24. Heather Gaunt, 'Identity and Nation in the Australian Public Library: The Development of Local and National Collections 1850s–1940s, Using the Tasmanian Public Library as Case Study' (PhD diss., University of Tasmania, 2010), 157, accessed August 6, 2018: https://eprints.utas.edu.au/10772/2/Gaunt_whole.pdf.

25. Gaunt, 'Identity and Nation in the Australian Public Library', 45.
26. Joshi, *In Another Country*, 53, 54, 55.
27. Wayne A. Weigand, *Part of our Lives: A People's History of The American Public Library* (Oxford: Oxford University Press, 2015), 25–26, 28, 48.
28. A 1859 letter in an unidentified newspaper in *Newspaper Cuttings Relating to the State Library of Victoria*, cited in McVilly, '"Something to Blow About"?', 89.

Open Access This chapter is licensed under the terms of the Creative Commons Attribution 4.0 International License (http://creativecommons.org/licenses/by/4.0/), which permits use, sharing, adaptation, distribution and reproduction in any medium or format, as long as you give appropriate credit to the original author(s) and the source, provide a link to the Creative Commons licence and indicate if changes were made.

The images or other third party material in this chapter are included in the chapter's Creative Commons licence, unless indicated otherwise in a credit line to the material. If material is not included in the chapter's Creative Commons licence and your intended use is not permitted by statutory regulation or exceeds the permitted use, you will need to obtain permission directly from the copyright holder.

Appendix A: Explanatory Note on Catalogue Sources

SAPL

There are 21 catalogues from the SAPL in the BCCSH digital archive. General catalogues of the library's complete holdings, printed in Cape Town, were issued in 1825, 1829, 1834, 1842, and 1862. Supplementary catalogues of annual additions were produced from the 1830s onwards. The SAPL catalogues have unusually detailed bibliographical information. Each major catalogue is divided into classes, and titles are listed by author, title, date of publication, and number of volumes within each class. The supplementary catalogues are listed by author and title, and provide the number of additional volumes acquired in each of the library's main subject classes. As well as the general SAPL catalogues, the archive includes separate catalogues of significant private bequests to the SAPL: the Dessinian Collection (1821) and Sir George Grey's Philological (1858) and Early Printed Books (1867) Collections.

MPL

The BCCSH archive includes 17 printed catalogues of the MPL ranging from 1854 to 1867. Between 1854 and 1861, these catalogues were lists of recent additions printed in London by the library's bookseller J. J. Guillaume. Printed in Melbourne, the 1861 catalogue is the first complete catalogue of the MPL and lists 26,723 volumes. Like the BML catalogues from 1849 onwards, the 1861 catalogue is arranged alphabetically by author and title rather than being classically divided. The catalogue features detailed information about the collection, including the date, place, and format of publication, and includes a classificatory index. A supplementary catalogue, listing additions to 1865, is arranged in the same fashion. A catalogue listing the extensive donations the library received from individuals and institutions across Europe appeared in 1867.

SAI

The 1848 SALMI catalogue is divided into 28 classes. Works are recorded by short title and number of volumes only, without further publication details. The 1851 catalogue has 25 classes. The catalogue contains some inconsistencies: for example, titles are sometimes listed alphabetically by author or title (see Novels), and sometimes by subject (see History). After the SAI was established in 1861, a full catalogue of the collection was printed by the government printer. The 1863 catalogue is a reissue of the 1861 catalogue with a small supplementary catalogue. The 1861/1863 catalogue is divided into 20 generic classes. The 1869 catalogue is also divided into 20 classes and the books in each class are primarily arranged alphabetically.

SL AND RLM

The 1860 SL catalogue, printed in Singapore by the Mission Press, divides the collection into six classes. Titles are numbered and listed by short title, author, and number of volumes. The 1863 catalogue, printed in Singapore by the library, is similarly classified. The only available printed catalogue of the RLM falling in the time-frame of this study is the 1877 catalogue. Printed in Singapore by the library, the catalogue's alphabetical listing is accompanied by a classificatory index separating the library's collection into 24 classes. Each class is marked with a letter. A list of subjects and the classificatory letter to which they correspond is also provided.

ASL AND FPL

The BCCSH archive includes 17 printed catalogues issued by the ASL, but the bibliographical rigour of these catalogues varies significantly. From 1828 to 1836, the ASL catalogues were poorly printed, unclassified author-title lists of the books in the collection. Three full classified catalogues of the library collection were issued in 1838, 1839, and 1843, with a further classified catalogue issued in 1853 styled as 'Part II' of the 1843 catalogue (representing the additions over the previous decade). Annual supplementary catalogues of recent additions appeared regularly in the 1840s, but the ASL's precarious financial position meant that only one such catalogue of recent additions was issued thereafter, in 1866. A final list of the ASL's collection was produced for the handover to the FPL in 1869.

TPL

A basic author-title catalogue printed in Hobart in 1849 shortly after the inauguration of the institution shows a modest collection, though it was soon greatly increased by the purchase of the bequest of James Bicheno in 1851. A catalogue printed in 1852 classifies the collection within 16 generic classes, and separates the books from the Bicheno bequest from the general collection within each of these categories. The next catalogue, issued in 1855, dispenses with the separation of the Bicheno books from the rest of collection, and expands the classificatory system from 16 to 34 classes, interspersing the classified subject sections with a general alphabetical list of the collection arranged by author-title. An 1862 catalogue of the TPL abandons the classification of the collection altogether and returns to an author-title alphabetical list along the lines of the (by then) fashionable BML catalogues.

Appendix B: Volume Numbers of Colonial Public Libraries

Year	ASL	MPL	SAI	SAPL	SI/RLM
1833	–	–	–	26,000	–
1842	–	–	–	30,000	–
1843	–	–	–	–	633
1845	–	–	–	–	895
1852	14,858	–	–	–	–
1853	–	–	–	32,000	–
1856	–	3846	–	–	–
1859	16,000	–	7356	–	–
1860	–	–	8187	–	–
1861	–	26,723	10,142	–	–
1862	–	–	11,142	–	–
1863	–	–	12,291	–	–
1864	–	–	12,344	–	–
1865	–	34,000	12,031	–	–
1866	16,000	–	12,885	–	–
1867	–	–	14,040	–	–
1868	–	–	14,048	–	–
1869	16,000	–	14,879	–	–
1870	–	57,370	15,559	–	–
1874	–	–	–	–	3000

Appendix C: Genre Proportions of Colonial Public Libraries by Title

Table C.1 SL and RLM

Year	Biography and History	Imaginative Literature	Geography, Voyages, and Travel	Political Economy, Politics, and Jurisprudence	Science	Theology and Ethics	Other
1860	31%	44%	11%	0%	0%	2%	12%
1863	36%	36%	12%	0%	0%	2%	14%
1877	24%	28%	28%	1%	7%	3%	9%

Table C.2 SAI

Year	Biography and History	Imaginative Literature	Geography, Voyages, and Travel	Political Economy, Politics, and Jurisprudence	Science	Theology and Ethics	Other
1848	18%	16%	14%	5%	15%	4%	28%
1851	15%	36%	11%	4%	8%	2%	24%
1861	13%	37%	12%	2%	8%	2%	26%
1863[a]	16%	25%	14%	3%	9%	3%	30%
1869	14%	27%	14%	2%	11%	3%	29%

[a]Indicates supplementary catalogues

© The Author(s) 2019
L. Atkin et al., *Early Public Libraries and Colonial Citizenship in the British Southern Hemisphere*, New Directions in Book History,
https://doi.org/10.1007/978-3-030-20426-6

Table C.3 SAPL

Year	Biography and History	Imaginative Literature	Geography, Voyages, and Travel	Political Economy, Politics, and Jurisprudence	Science	Theology and Ethics	Other
1825	14%	11%	28%	24%	6%	0%	17%
1829	21%	4%	12%	10%	21%	4%	28%
1834	11%	12%	12%	10%	17%	6%	32%
1842	17%	13%	11%	6%	12%	6%	35%
1862	29%	17%	18%	5%	14%	7%	10%

Table C.4 ASL

Year	Biography and History	Imaginative Literature	Geography, Voyages, and Travel	Political Economy, Politics, and Jurisprudence	Science	Theology and Ethics	Other
1839	20%	29%	14%	6%	7%	7%	18%
1840[a]	29%	26%	14%	5%	8%	7%	11%
1841[a]	23%	22%	13%	14%	5%	9%	14%
1842[a]	18%	26%	10%	7%	3%	9%	27%
1843	21%	30%	14%	6%	8%	8%	13%
1845[a]	18%	33%	18%	5%	6%	3%	17%
1847[a]	23%	21%	23%	3%	5%	3%	22%
1850[a]	25%	18%	26%	3%	6%	2%	20%
1853	21%	28%	16%	5%	6%	6%	18%

[a]Indicates supplementary catalogues

Table C.5 TPL

Year	Biography and History	Imaginative Literature	Geography, Voyages, and Travel	Political Economy, Politics, and Jurisprudence	Science	Theology and Ethics	Other
1852	28%	12%	12%	2%	13%	4%	29%
1855	21%	16%	22%	5%	13%	6%	17%

Table C.6 MPL

Year	Biography and History	Imaginative Literature	Geography, Voyages, and Travel	Political Economy, Politics, and Jurisprudence	Science	Theology and Ethics	Other
1861	31%	5%	9%	9%	12%	5%	29%

Select Bibliography

Altick, Richard D. *The English Common Reader: A Social History of the Mass Reading Public, 1800–1900*. Chicago: University of Chicago Press, 1957.
Ballantyne, Tony. *Webs of Empire: Locating New Zealand's Colonial Past*. Vancouver: UBC Press, 2012.
Belich, James. *Replenishing the Earth: The Settler Revolution and the Rise of the Anglo-World, 1783–1939*. Oxford: Oxford University Press, 2009.
Black, Alistair. 'The People's University: Models of Public Library History'. In Black and Hoare, *Cambridge History of Libraries in Great Britain and Ireland Volume III*, 24–39.
Black, Alistair, and Peter Hoare, ed. *The Cambridge History of Libraries in Great Britain and Ireland Volume III 1850–2000*. Cambridge: Cambridge University Press, 2006.
Cavallo, Guglielmo, and Roger Chartier, ed. *A History of Reading in the West*. Trans. Lydia G. Cochrane. Amherst: University of Michigan, 1997.
Dick, Archie L. 'Book History, Library History and South Africa's Reading Culture'. *South African Historical Journal* 55, no. 1 (2006): 33–45.
Dubow, Saul. *The Commonwealth of Knowledge: Science, Sensibility, and White South Africa, 1820–2000*. Oxford: Oxford University Press, 2006.
Errington, Joseph. *Linguistics in a Colonial World: A Story of Language, Meaning and Power*. Malden MA and Oxford: Blackwell, 2008.
Fischer-Tiné, Harald. 'Britain's Other Civilising Mission: Class Prejudice, European "Loaferism" and the Workhouse-system in Colonial India'. *The Indian Economic and Social History Review* 42, no. 3 (2005): 295–338.
Flint, Kate. *The Woman Reader, 1837–1914*. Oxford: Clarendon Press, 1993.

Friis, Theodorus. *The Public Library in South Africa: An Evaluative Study.* Cape Town: Afrikaanse Pers-Boekhandel, 1962.

Gaunt, Heather. 'Identity and Nation in the Australian Public Library: The Development of Local and National Collections 1850s–1940s, Using the Tasmanian Public Library as Case Study'. PhD diss., University of Tasmania, 2010.

Gilmour, Rachael. *Grammars of Colonialism: Representing Languages in Colonial South Africa.* Basingstoke: Palgrave, 2006.

Hammond, Mary. '"The Great Fiction Bore": Free Libraries and the Construction of a Reading Public in England, 1880–1914'. *Libraries & Culture* 37, no. 2 (Spring 2002): 83–108.

Han, Lim Peng. 'The Beginning and Development of the Raffles Library in Singapore, 1823–1941: A Nineteenth-Century and Early Twentieth-Century British Colonial Enclave'. *Library and Information History* 25, no. 4 (2009): 265–278.

Hofmeyr, Isabel. 'The Globe in the Text: Towards a Transnational History of the Book'. *African Studies* 64, no. 1 (2005): 87–103.

Innes, Joanne. 'Libraries in Context; Social, Cultural and Intellectual Background'. In Mandelbrote and Manley, *Cambridge History of Libraries in Britain and Ireland Volume II*, 285–300.

Joshi, Priya. *In Another County: Colonialism, Culture and the English Novel in India.* New York: Columbia University Press, 2002.

Joyce, Patrick. 'The Politics of the Liberal Archive'. *History of the Human Sciences* 12, no. 3 (1999): 35–49.

Kerr, Donald J. *Amassing Treasures for All Time: Sir George Grey, Colonial Bookman and Collector.* Dunedin: Otago University Press, 2006.

Kerr, Donald J. '"Building Monuments More Enduring than Brass": Governor Sir George Grey, a Study of his Book Collection and the Formation of his Libraries'. PhD diss., University of Auckland, 2001.

Kirsop, Wallace. 'Libraries for an Imperial Power'. In Mandelbrote and Manley, *Cambridge History of Libraries in Britain and Ireland Volume II*, 494–508.

Kirsop, Wallace. 'Redmond Barry and the Libraries'. *La Trobe Journal* 73 (2004): 55–66.

Kirsop, Wallace. 'Writing a History of Nineteenth-Century Commercial Circulating Libraries: Problems and Possibilities'. *Bibliographical Society of Australia and New Zealand Bulletin* 27 (2003): 71–82.

Lamond, Julieanne. 'Communities of Readers: Australian Reading History and Library Loan Records'. In *Republics of Letters: Literary Communities in Australia*, ed. Peter Kirkpatrick and Robert Dixon, 27–38. Sydney: University of Sydney Press.

Lester, Alan. 'Settler Colonialism, George Grey and the Politics of Ethnography'. *Environmental and Planning D: Society and Space* 34, no. 3 (2016): 492–507.

Levett, John. 'The Tasmanian Public Library 1849–1869: The Rise and Fall of a Colonial Institution'. MA thesis, Monash University, 1984.

Livingstone, David N. *Putting Science in its Place: Geographies of Scientific Knowledge*. Chicago: University of Chicago Press, 2003.

Luyt, Brendan. 'Centres of Calculation and Unruly Colonists: The Colonial Library in Singapore and its Users, 1874–1900'. *Journal of Documentation* (2008): 386–396.

Luyt, Brendan. 'The Importance of Fiction to the Raffles Library, Singapore, During the Long Nineteenth-Century'. *Library & Information History* 25, no. 2 (2009): 117–131.

Mandelbrote, Giles, and K. A. Manley, ed. *The Cambridge History of Libraries in Britain and Ireland Volume II: 1640–1850*. Cambridge: Cambridge University Press, 2006.

MacMahon, Richard. 'The History of Transdisciplinary Race Classification: Methods, Politics and Institutions, 1840s–1940s'. *British Journal of History of Science* 51, no. 1 (2018): 41–67.

McVilly, David. 'A History of the State Library of Victoria, 1853–1974'. MA thesis, Monash University, 1975.

McVilly, David. '"Something to Blow About"?—the State Library of Victoria, 1856–1880'. *La Trobe Journal* 8 (1971): 81–90.

Moran, Shane. *Representing Bushmen: South Africa and the Origin of Language*. Cambridge: Cambridge University Press, 2009.

Qureshi, Sadiah. 'Robert Gordon Latham, Displayed Peoples, and the Natural History of Race, 1854–1866'. *The Historical Journal* 54, no. 1 (March 2011a): 143–166.

Qureshi, Sadiah. *Peoples on Parade: Exhibitions, Empire and Anthropology in Nineteenth-Century Britain*. Chicago: University of Chicago Press, 2011b.

Raven, James. 'Libraries for Sociability: The Advance of the Subscription Library'. In Mandelbrote and Manley, *Cambridge History of Libraries in Britain and Ireland Volume II*, 239–263.

Reynolds, Sue. 'Libraries, Librarians, and Librarianship in the Colony of Victoria'. *Australian Academic and Research Libraries* 40, no. 1 (2013): 50–64.

Roberts, Kyle B., and Mark Towsey, ed. *Before the Public Library: Reading, Community, and Identity in the Atlantic World, 1650–1850*. Leiden and Boston: Brill, 2018.

Roberts, Lewis C. 'Disciplining and Disinfecting Working-Class Readers in the Victorian Public Library'. *Victorian Literature and Culture* 26, no. 1 (1998): 105–132.

Rudy, Jason R. *Imagined Homelands: British Poetry in the Colonies*. Baltimore: Johns Hopkins University Press, 2017.

Spevack, Marvin. 'The Impact of the British Museum Library'. In Mandelbrote and Manley, *Cambridge History of Libraries in Britain and Ireland Volume II*, 422–37.

Stoler, Ann L. *Carnal Knowledge and Imperial Power: Race and the Invention of Colonial Rule*. Berkeley: University of California Press, 2002.

Talbot, Michael. 'A Close Affiliation: Coordination of Institutes in South Australia'. In *Pioneering Culture: Mechanics Institutes and Schools of Art in Australia*, edited by P. C. Candy and J. Laurent, 335–56. Adelaide, Auslib Press, 1994

Traue, J. E. 'The Public Library Explosion in Colonial New Zealand'. *Libraries & the Cultural Record* 42, no. 2 (2007): 151–164.

Twidle, Hedley. 'From *The Origin of Language* to a Language of Origin: A Prologue to the Grey Collection'. In van der Vlies, *Print, Text and Book Cultures in South Africa*, 252–83.

Twidle, Hedley. '"The Bushmen's Letters": |Xam Narratives of the Bleek Lloyd Archive and their Afterlives'. In *The Cambridge History of South African Literature*, edited by David Attwell and Derek Attridge, 19–37. Cambridge: Cambridge University Press, 2012.

van der Vlies, Andrew, ed. *Print, Text and Book Cultures in South Africa*. Johannesburg: Wits University Press, 2012.

Warner, Michael. *Publics and Counterpublics*. New York: Zone Books, 2002.

Weigand, Wayne A. *Part of our Lives: A People's History of The American Public Library*. Oxford: Oxford University Press, 2015.

Index[1]

A

Aborigines (Australian), 14n15, 107, 133
Adamson, James, 27, 79
Adelaide, 21, 129
Adelaide Circulating Library, 88
Advocate's Library (Edinburgh), 10
Africa, 96, 104, 110, 119
Ainsworth, William Harrison, 92
Albany, 115
America, 10, 28, 134, 135
Anglo-divergence, 2
Anglophone, 2, 28, 30, 67, 68, 95, 111, 112, 128
Anglosphere, 3, 12, 21
Anglo-world, 104, 113, 116
Anthropological Society (London), 107
Anthropology, 106, 107, 111, 118
Asiatic Society of Bengal, 111
Auckland, 4, 116, 120
Auckland Public Library, 5, 115
Austin, Sarah, 86
Australia, 2, 4, 5, 11, 13n2, 14n15, 19–21, 25, 30, 34, 35, 47, 49, 104, 107, 114–116, 119, 120, 132–135
Australian Subscription Library (ASL), 7, 11, 19, 21, 23, 29, 34, 58, 59, 79, 84, 85, 92, 93, 96, 130, 140–141, 146

B

Bacon, Francis, 88
Bain, James, 35
Ballarat Free Public Library, 30, 51
Barkly, Henry, 96
Barnard, Edward, 85–87, 92
Barrow, John, 109
Barry, Redmond, 4, 22, 23, 29, 30, 32, 33, 35, 36, 50, 51, 54, 85, 86, 90, 107, 133
Basevi, George, 31
Batavia, 112

---

[1] Note: Page numbers followed by 'n' refer to notes.

© The Author(s) 2019
L. Atkin et al., *Early Public Libraries and Colonial Citizenship in the British Southern Hemisphere*, New Directions in Book History, https://doi.org/10.1007/978-3-030-20426-6

Batavian Society of Arts and Sciences, 111, 112
Bateman, Edward La Trobe, 93, 94
Bicheno collection, 85, 96
Bicheno, James Ebenezer, 85, 96, 98n32, 141
Biography, 79, 88, 133
Bleek, Wilhelm, 107, 116–121, 133
Blumenbach, Johann Friedrich, 109
Bodleian Library (Oxford), 10
Bombay, 112
Bombay General Library, 132
Braddon, Mary Elizabeth, 59
Brayley, Edward William, 92
Bremer, Fredrika, 92
Bride, Thomas Francis, 57
Britain, 2, 4, 7, 12, 17, 18, 22, 25, 28, 29, 31, 36, 45, 47, 52–54, 65, 86, 89, 107–111, 119, 121, 128, 132–134
British Museum Library (BML), 10, 15n39, 16n49, 24, 29, 30, 32, 47, 56, 94, 139, 141
Brockhaus, F. A., 117
Brontë, Charlotte, 86
Brooks, Frederick, 90
Brunet, Jacques-Charles, 7, 93
Buffon, Comte de, 109
Bulwer-Lytton, Edward, 92, 132
Byron, George Gordon (Lord), 24

C
Calcutta, 112, 132
Calcutta Public Library, 132, 134
Calvert, Samuel, 32, 94
Canada, 28
Cape Colony, 2, 4, 5, 9, 11, 13n2, 19, 20, 24–27, 48, 61, 66, 68, 81, 83, 110–112, 116, 127, 128, 131, 134, 135
Cape Town, 2, 9, 12, 26, 48, 66, 79, 110, 116, 117, 121, 133, 134, 139

Capitalism, 30
Centre of calculation, 113, 117, 121
Ceylon, 112
Chetham's Library (Manchester), 28
Circulating libraries, 11, 20, 24, 31, 47, 54, 66, 81, 83, 87, 88, 132
Citizenship, 2, 12, 45, 46, 135
Clarke, Andrew, 63
Colonies
 British, 1
 franchise, 48, 134
 southern, 1, 4, 9–11, 18–21, 24, 31, 36, 46, 48, 55, 61, 68, 78, 79, 81, 83, 91, 93, 96, 105–108, 114, 128, 130–134
Combe, George, 106
Community libraries, 1, 17–36
Comparative, 3, 8, 9, 33, 105–109, 115–118, 133
Comparativism, 3
Cooper, Charles, 87, 89
Cooper, James Fenimore, 92
Cowper, William, 88
Cull, Richard, 112
Cultural capital, 2, 7, 31, 104, 117, 129

D
Darwin, Charles, 114, 115, 119
Defoe, Daniel, 92
Dessin, Joachim Nicolaas von, 96, 131
Dessinian Collection, 10, 67, 96, 131, 139
Dickens, Charles, 24, 87, 92, 132
Disraeli, Benjamin, 92, 133
Drummond Jervois, W. F., 129, 130
Dublin, 31
Du Cane, Charles, 18
Duffy, Charles Gavan, 35
Dwight, H. T., 36

INDEX 155

E
Edgeworth, Maria, 86, 92, 133
Edinburgh, 10, 92, 112
Education
  home, 25–28, 78
  working-class, 20, 129, 131, 135
Eliot, George, 24
England, 10, 18, 28, 29, 31, 33, 35, 90, 91, 94, 96
Ethics, 51
Ethnography, 33, 34, 36, 115, 133
Ethnological Society (London), 107, 110, 111
Ethnology, 5, 105–111, 120, 122n16

F
Federation, 3, 19, 135
Fiction, 4, 5, 8, 52, 54, 78, 80, 81, 83–85, 87–92, 130, 132, 133, 136n23
Fiction problem, 5, 80
Fiji, 96
Fitzwilliam Museum (Cambridge), 31
Free Public Library (Sydney) (FPL), 8, 11, 21, 23, 34, 49, 62, 84, 85, 98n30, 130, 131, 133, 134, 136n23, 140–141

G
Geography, 8, 79
Gipps, George, 21
Global, 2–4, 10, 18, 22, 28, 108, 112, 117, 128, 129
Globalism, 3, 13n8
Gold rush, 30, 48, 55
Gore, Catherine, 86, 92
Governmentality, 120
Gray, Thomas, 88
Grey, George, 4, 9, 10, 96, 104, 107, 114, 124n59, 127, 128, 133, 139
Guillaume, J. J., 29, 35, 86, 106, 139

H
Haeckel, Ernst, 119
Hanson, Richard, 81
Hazlitt, William, 92
Herschel, John, 111
History, 2–6, 8, 26, 31, 33, 36, 46–48, 54, 67, 68, 79, 80, 83, 86, 88–90, 94, 105, 106, 108–110, 115, 122n9, 133, 140
Hobart, 12, 81, 82, 141
Hoëvell, W. R., Baron von, 112
Hole, James, 79
Holgate, C. W., 68
Hong Kong, 112
Horne, R. H., 91
Hose, F. R., 114
Hunt, James, 106, 107
Huxley, Thomas, 119

I
Imaginative literature, 8, 81–87
India, 9, 35, 84, 93, 111, 114, 132–134
Indigenous, 2, 5, 36, 46, 48, 63–69, 104, 110, 111, 114–121, 128, 133–135
Ireland, 17, 18, 47, 96

J
James, G. P. R., 92
Jameson, Anna, 86
Jardine, Alexander Johnstone, 7, 8, 33, 48, 52, 68, 88, 89, 93
Johnson, Samuel, 88
Journal of the Indian Archipelago and Eastern Asia (JIA), 111–114
Jurisprudence, 8, 82, 145–147

K
Knox, Robert, 106

L

Lang, John Dunmore, 79, 84, 130
Latham, Robert Gordon, 106
La Trobe, Charles Joseph, 85, 96
Lawrence, William, 109, 123n30
Leeds, 12, 80
Legal deposit, 24, 25, 35
Lever, Charles James, 92
Lewis, F. S., 66
Liberalism, 17–36
Librarians, 7, 20, 22, 23, 33, 34, 50–52, 57, 66, 80, 88, 89, 92, 95, 105, 106, 113, 133
Library committees, 21, 30, 33, 46, 47, 52, 58, 65, 78, 79, 89, 109, 130, 132
Linnaeus, Carl, 109
Literacy rates, 5, 47, 48, 91
Little, Robert, 26, 65, 83
Logan, James Richardson, 4, 5, 107, 108, 111–114, 133
London Institution, 7, 9, 92
Lowry-Corry, Somerset Richard (Earl of Belmore), 85
Lyell, Charles, 115, 119

M

Macaulay, Thomas Babington, 88
Madagascar, 116
Madras, 112
Madras Literary Society, 132
Malacca, 11, 26
Malay Archipelago, 33, 65, 133
Manchester, 12, 28, 51
Māori, 119, 120
Marryat, Frederick, 92, 132
Maskew, Frederick, 68, 105
Mauritius, 96
Mechanics' institutes, 9, 11, 12, 20, 21, 49, 55, 61, 83, 84, 87, 134

Melbourne, 2, 4, 10, 24, 28, 31, 35, 36, 49, 50, 53, 54, 56, 59, 87, 91, 94, 95, 121, 133, 134, 139
Milton, John, 24
Missionaries, 4, 66, 105, 108, 115, 116, 128, 132
Mission libraries, 134
Mitchell, David Scott, 34
Mitchell, Thomas, 96
Modernity
   accelerated, 30
   colonial, 30, 120
Molteno Regulations, 19, 66
Moscow, 31
Mudie's Circulating Library, 11, 132
Mullen, Samuel, 107
Muller, Frederik, 35
Müller, Max, 119
Musgrave, William, 79

N

Nationalism, 3
Nationhood, 3
Natural history, 33, 36, 67, 105, 106, 108, 115
Networks, 2, 4, 7, 20, 22, 66, 93, 108, 110–117, 119, 121, 125n59
Neumayer, Georg von, 96
New imperial history, 4
Newman, W. A., 26, 78
New South Wales, 19, 21, 25, 27, 28, 47, 55, 85, 131
New Zealand, 4, 5, 9, 10, 13n2, 19–21, 25, 27, 30, 34, 48, 95, 96, 98n22, 104, 114–116, 119, 120, 129
Nova Scotia, 27

O

Oliphant, Margaret, 86

P

Panizzi, Antonio, 24, 89, 94
Pasley, Charles, 96
Pauperism, 65
Penang Library, 11
Philology, 8, 33, 34, 105–107, 115, 117–120, 123n23, 133
Political economy, 8, 82, 145–147
Politics, 35, 67, 103
Popular Library (Cape Town), 48
Porter, William, 24, 60, 77, 78, 83
Press
  colonial, 19
  periodical, 33
Prichard, James Cowles, 106, 109–112
Public libraries
  access to, 12, 21–24, 29, 46, 52, 54, 63, 67, 84, 91, 94
  Acts (British), 12, 17, 20, 134
  admission policies of, 22, 29
  American, 10, 11, 52
  bequests to, 5
  British, 46, 62
  buildings of, 50, 62, 85, 114, 129
  catalogues of, 6, 7, 106
  censorship of, 52, 53
  and circulation, 6, 11, 46, 49, 82, 84
  cleanliness of, 51, 56
  collections/holdings of, 3, 6, 24, 80, 88, 96, 107, 114
  facilities/technologies of, 29, 31, 129
  genre proportions of, 4, 79, 80, 82, 145–147
  Indian, 68, 134
  municipal, 8, 11, 18, 19, 23, 45, 80, 132, 135
  opening hours of, 23, 29, 54, 134
  and reference, 9, 11, 47, 49, 81–83, 88, 111, 113, 129, 131, 133
  and surveillance, 51, 52
  and travelling libraries, 87
Public sphere, 2, 4, 5, 20, 135

Q

Quaritch, Bernard, 35
Queensland, 95
Queen Victoria, 12, 27, 28, 30, 31, 35, 47–49, 95, 108, 127

R

Raffles Library and Museum (RLM), 5, 8, 9, 11, 21, 23, 26, 32, 34, 48, 52, 62, 63, 65, 68, 83, 84, 88, 105, 112, 113, 132–134, 140
Raffles, Stamford, 65
Readers
  female, 58–69
  indigenous, 67, 134
  lounger/loafer, 46
  middle class, 47–53, 56
  non-British (German, Dutch etc.), 63–69
  working-class, 48–50
Reading
  communities, 5, 6, 46
  curative role of, 26
  history of, 6
  light/serious, 26, 27, 53, 63, 81, 90, 91
  publics, 21, 61
Rees, Rowland, 24, 131
Responsible government, 3, 27, 89, 97, 131, 135
Richardson, James Malcott, 10, 11, 92, 132, 133
Ross, Robert, 79
Rost, Reinhold, 113
Royal Geographical Society (London), 111

S

San people, 110, 118
Science, 8, 12, 25, 28, 49, 59, 79, 80, 82, 84–86, 88, 104–111, 113, 115, 117, 120, 121, 129, 133
Scotland, 10
Scott, Walter, 56, 80, 91, 92, 132, 133
Self-governance, 2, 27, 135
Selwyn, George Augustus, 116
Sheridan, Richard Brinsley, 61
Singapore, 2, 4, 5, 11, 19, 25, 26, 30, 48, 52, 62, 63, 66, 68, 81, 83, 105, 108, 111–113, 121, 132, 133, 135, 140
Singapore Library (SL), 11, 19, 21, 48, 51, 60, 62, 68, 81, 83, 90, 91, 93, 105, 108, 111, 132, 140
Smith, Elder & Co., 10, 11, 93, 132
Smith, Harry, 27, 61
Society of Antiquaries, 95
South Africa, 20, 25, 28, 33, 104, 114, 115, 117, 118, 129, 134
South African College, 27
South African Museum (SAM), 10, 108, 109
South African Public Library (SAPL), 5, 7–11, 20, 22, 23, 25–29, 31, 33, 48, 56, 59–61, 66–68, 77, 79, 81–83, 88, 89, 92, 93, 96, 104–106, 108–111, 115–117, 127–129, 131–133, 139
South African Quarterly Journal (SAQJ), 110–112
South Australia, 12, 25, 31, 47, 67, 88, 90, 108, 114, 120, 129, 130
South Australian Institute (SAI), 8, 11, 12, 19, 21, 23, 24, 28–32, 34, 47, 49, 51, 52, 61, 67, 81, 83, 84, 87–89, 94, 105, 106, 108, 131, 133, 134, 140
South Australian Library and Mechanics' Institute (SALMI), 11, 21, 22, 34, 56, 83, 92, 93, 140
Southeast Asia, 93, 112, 114, 133, 134
Sotheran, Henry, 35
Southern Africa, 110, 116–118, 128
Southern African people, 110, 111, 117
See also San people
Southern hemisphere, 1, 4, 6, 48, 91, 106, 134, 135
Stowe, Harriet Beecher, 81
Straits Branch of the Royal Asiatic Society, 33–34, 113, 114, 133
Straits Settlements, 1, 2, 4, 9, 19, 20, 25, 63, 111, 112, 128–130, 132
Subscription libraries, 9, 11, 12, 19, 20, 45, 59, 60, 82, 83, 85, 87, 88, 91, 133, 134
Swinburne, Algernon Charles, 24
Sydney, 11, 21, 47, 49, 62, 91, 93, 130, 131

T

Tasmania, 12, 18, 28, 48, 95, 96
Tasmanian Public Library (TPL), 8, 12, 18, 23, 34, 48, 59, 61, 68, 69, 85, 96, 98n32, 132, 141
Tennyson, Alfred (Lord), 24
Thackeray, William Makepeace, 24, 87, 92
Theology, 8, 145–147
Toronto, 31
Transnationalism, 3, 93, 110, 112, 116
Travels, 33, 35, 67, 118
Trollope, Frances, 86, 92
Trübner & Co., 119
Tulk, Augustus, 52, 95, 106–107

U
United States (US), 28, 81, 96

V
Victoria
  colony of, 27, 28, 86, 89, 94, 131
  Queen (*see* Queen Victoria)
Voyages, 33, 67, 115, 118

W
Wellington, 9

Western Australia, 27, 115
White, Canon, 80, 81, 88, 89
Wiremu Maihi Te Rangikaheke, 120
Wylde, John, 26

Y
Yorkshire Union of Mechanics' Institutes, 11

Z
Zoology, 106, 109, 110

The manufacturer's authorised representative in the EU is Springer Nature Customer Service Centre GmbH, Europaplatz 3, 69115 Heidelberg, Germany. If you have any concerns regarding our products, please contact ProductSafety@springernature.com

Printed and bound by CPI Group (UK) Ltd, Croydon, CR0 4YY
23/03/2026
02076402-0013